iPhone Manual for Beginners

2nd Edition (iOS 11 & 10)

Covers iPhones: 8, 8 Plus, 7, 7 Plus, 6s, 6s Plus, 6, 6 Plus, 5s, 5c, 5, & SE

Joe Malacina

An Infinity Guides book

InfinityGuides.com

iPhone Manual for Beginners

Trademarks & Acknowledgements

Warning & Disclaimer

Contact the Publisher

To contact No Limit Enterprises, Inc. or the author for sales, marketing material, or any commercial purpose, please visit www.nolimitcorp.com, or e-mail info@nolimitcorp.com.

iPhone® Manual for Beginners, 2nd Edition
Publisher: No Limit Enterprises, Inc.
Author: Joe Malacina
ISBN: 978-0-9989196-4-5
Library of Congress Control Number: 2018902714
Printed in the U.S.A.

TABLE OF CONTENTS

INTRODUCTION

Congratulations! So you have decided to take the first step, in fact the only step needed to learn how to use your iPhone. Maybe you don't even have an iPhone yet, and just want to see how it works before you decide whether to buy one. Either way, this book will teach you everything you need to know on using your iPhone. I wanted to take this time to tell you how this book is going to be the only thing you will ever need in order to learn your iPhone. You see, this book was written for the perspective of a beginner. In other words, if you have never used a "smartphone" in your life, that will be no detriment when reading this book. That is the big difference between this book and other competitors available. Many authors fail to realize that even in 2017, many people are buying their first "smartphone," and need to be shown from the ground up the basics of using and navigating their device. So that is what this book sets out to accomplish. I teach you not only how to do specific functions on your iPhone, but I will teach you the building blocks of using any "smart" device. When you are finished reading this book, not only will you be a pro using your iPhone, you will be able to pick up any smartphone or tablet and have a general understanding of how it works and how to accomplish tasks.

This book is structured so that basic concepts I teach you in beginning chapters will be used in later chapters. Therefore, I highly recommend reading the first few chapters, instead of skipping ahead to exactly what you want to learn. You may miss out on essential tidbits of information that I will not cover in detail in later chapters.

Lastly, you may be wondering if this book is suitable for you. Will it answer all the questions you have? Will you understand the material? I can assure you that the information addressed in this book is derived directly from the input of several thousand iPhone users who have had the same questions as you. I have been teaching people how to use their iPhone for over 3 years, and have taught well over 50,000 people of all ages and backgrounds how to use their devices. I have run a blog and numerous websites where I have received over 10,000 e-mails with questions on how to do this and how to do that. So I can assure you, I know what the most common questions are, and where the most confusion lies. So take solace in the fact that this book will address your questions with a step-by-step approach, while building your technological intuition. When you are done, you will not even need to memorize the steps to perform a function, you will have the intuition and knowledge to figure it out quickly. That is the core of what this book will teach you.

This being the 2nd edition of the *iPhone Manual for Beginners*, every chapter has been updated to better explain and demonstrate the different functions of the iPhone. We have also updated every illustration and revamped the appendixes. As always, I welcome your feedback on this book and you can always reach me on Twitter @JoeMalacina.

On a final note, Apple users, particularly iPhone users, are notoriously loyal to their cell phones, and tend to keep using iPhones each coming year. After reading this book, you may start to see exactly why. The iPhone interface and navigation is seamless and soon you will find yourself liking the way it does things. Soon after that, you will notice that many other Apple devices work in very similar ways, and may find yourself wanting to explore other Apple devices such an iPad or Mac. If you ever find yourself wondering how these devices work, I urge you to check out www.infinityguides.com. There you can find beginners' books, manuals, and online courses on many Apple devices.

On that introduction, let us get started

Chapter 1 – About the iPhone

So you now have an iPhone and you're ready to start using it. So what is a new iPhone exactly? Your iPhone is classified as a smartphone, which means that it can do everything a cell phone can do, plus additional features. So with your iPhone, you can make and receive calls, browse the internet, send text messages, check your email, and use apps. You can do all this with a phone that utilizes a touch screen. Before I show you how to do all these tasks, let's familiarize ourselves with some key terms that I will use often in this book. These terms are important for you to remember, as you will encounter them often.

Key Terms

Apple ID – Let's get the trickiest one out of the way early. By far, the most common question I receive is about the Apple ID. Let me define exactly what an Apple ID is. If you have ever used an Apple device before, such as a Mac computer or iPad, you have probably encountered the term Apple ID before. An Apple ID is just an e-mail address that is associated with you and your Apple devices. You need only one Apple ID, and you can use that same Apple ID on all of your Apple devices. I will go into creating an Apple ID in a chapter coming up, but for now just know that your Apple ID is your account that you will use on your iPhone. This account saves all of your important data such as contacts, photos, and your purchases.

Apps – Apps are programs on your iPhone that can do tasks. Your iPhone comes with many apps already installed, and you can download many more through the App Store. Nearly every aspect within the iPhone is part of an app, which you will see later on. Apps appear as square icons on your iPhone's home screen. (See Figure 1.1).

iTunes – iTunes is an app and a piece of software that is used to manage your iPhone's settings. There is an app on your iPhone called iTunes, where you can purchase and download music. More importantly, you can and should download iTunes on one of your computers. iTunes software on a computer backs up your iPhone's data every time you plug it in, and iTunes can be used to reset your iPhone in case there is a major problem with it. It is not necessary, but highly recommended that you download and install iTunes on one of your computers. Instructions on how to download iTunes can be found on the website www.applevideoguides.com/itunes-install.html.

Home Screen – Throughout this book, you will see the term home screen used often. Your home screen is the main screen of your iPhone where all of your Apps are shown.

Portrait & Landscape – You can view your iPhone in portrait or landscape mode. Portrait mode is the standard mode where your home button is on the bottom. Landscape mode is when you turn your iPhone horizontal, and the content of your iPhone also becomes horizontally oriented. Many apps allow you to use your iPhone in landscape mode and some require it. Just know that you can change the orientation of your iPhone at any time, and many apps allow you to do so.

Different iPhones & iOS

There are many different iPhones out in the marketplace, and it is important to understand the main differences between them. The reason this is important is so you understand why this book works for nearly all iPhones, and here it is: All iPhones operate nearly exactly the same, depending upon which software they are using. So if you have an iPhone 8, and your friend has an iPhone 6, they will operate in almost the exact same way in every single aspect as long as both iPhones are using the same software version. The only differences between iPhones are where some buttons are located, such as the power button, and the hardware underneath the iPhone. Some older iPhones will have different charging ports as well. All in all, remember this: No matter which iPhone you have, it will work nearly the same as every other iPhone that is running the same software.

Let's now explain the software running on iPhones. The software your iPhone is running is called its iOS. iOS stands for I Operating System, and it governs how everything in your iPhone works. iOS is labeled by a number, and the higher the number, the newer the software. For instance, the iPhone 8 comes with iOS 11. The iPhone 6S originally came with iOS 9. At all times you should be using the newest version of iOS available for your iPhone. So if you have an iPhone 6S with iOS 9, you should update the software to iOS 11. I show you how to update the software in Chapter 3.

All of these square icons are apps

Figure 1.1 – The Home Screen

Chapter 2 – iPhone Layout

Now we enter the "instruction manual" portion of this book, and we start with the iPhone layout. Shown in <u>Figure 2.1</u> is the layout of an iPhone 8.

Figure 2.1 – Layout of iPhone

As you can see, the power button is on the right side of the phone, while the volume buttons are on the left. On older iPhones, the power button will be on the top of the iPhone near the right. Pressing the power button turns the iPhone on when the phone is off. When the iPhone is already on, pressing the power button turns the screen on or off. The volume buttons are used to control the volume of the iPhone. Pressing the top volume button increases the iPhone volume, while pressing the bottom volume button decreases volume. Above the volume buttons is the vibrate switch. When the switch is flipped up, sound mode is on for the iPhone, which means your iPhone will ring when called and play sounds. When you flip the vibrate switch down, this turns on vibrate mode. In this mode, the iPhone will not ring, and will not make sounds.

Looking at the front of the iPhone, we have the most important button, the home button. The home button is the circular button on the front of the iPhone near the bottom. Pressing this button at any time will ALWAYS return you to your home screen. So if you are inside an app and need to go to your home screen, pressing the home button will accomplish that. Also on the front of the iPhone near the top, you can see a small circle which is the front facing camera.

At the bottom of your iPhone is the charging port. On older iPhones this will be a wider port than on newer iPhones. This port is called the lightning connector port, and allows you to charge your iPhone, connect accessories, and connect your iPhone to other devices.

On the back of your iPhone is the rear camera and the flash.

Turning your iPhone on and off

When your iPhone is off, you can turn it on by pressing and holding the power button until your screen lights up. This will turn your iPhone on and it will start booting up. After several seconds it will boot up completely.

At any time you can turn your iPhone off by pressing and holding the power button until Figure 2.2 appears. To turn your iPhone off from this screen, place your finger down on the red power symbol, and slide it across to the right, releasing at the end. This turns your iPhone off.

To turn iPhone off from this screen: Tap on the power icon with your finger, hold down, then swipe your finger to the right, releasing at the end.

Figure 2.2 – Power iPhone off

Charging your iPhone

To charge your iPhone, plug the included USB cable into the bottom of your iPhone, and connect the opposite end (USB) into a USB port or charging dock. Any powered USB port will charge your iPhone including USB ports on your computer or vehicle. The charging dock can be plugged into an electrical outlet. Once your iPhone is fully charged, you should disconnect the charging cable. For best battery life, the best practice you can follow is letting your iPhone's battery drain to yellow or red levels, then charge it until it is full, followed by unplugging the charging cable.

On the iPhone 8 and 8 Plus, you can charge your iPhone wirelessly by using a wireless charging pad. To do this, simply place the back of your iPhone onto the charging pad, and it will begin to charge without you having to plug anything into the iPhone. Wireless charging pads are a separate accessory that are not currently included with the iPhone 8 or 8 Plus.

Chapter 3 – Getting Started

This chapter covers getting started with your iPhone, and goes over the first-time setup procedure. If you have already completed the first-time setup where you chose your language and created your Apple ID you can skip the first part of this chapter.

First-time Setup

When you power on your iPhone for the very first time (press and hold the power button when the iPhone is off), you will be brought to the first-time setup screen shown in <u>Figure 3.1</u>. This first screen will say Hello in multiple languages. Here are the steps required to move past the initial setup successfully.

1. On the Hello screen (<u>Figure 3.1</u>), press the <u>home button</u> one time to move to the next screen. Or, you may need to tap down on the screen with your finger, and swipe your finger to the right to begin.

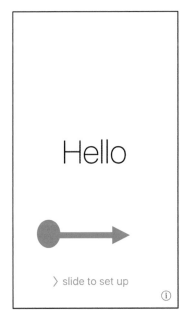

To move to the next screen, tap down on the screen with your finger, hold it there, and slide your finger to the right, and release your finger at the end. This is called a swipe.

<u>Figure 3.1</u> – Hello Screen

2. You are now asked to select your language (<u>Figure 3.2</u>). Tap with your finger one time on the language you wish to use for your iPhone. If your language doesn't appear, tap down on the screen and move your finger up and down to scroll through the list of languages. Release your finger to complete the scroll.

To choose your language, you can tap down on the screen with your finger, and move your finger up and down the screen to "scroll" through different choices. When "scrolling", remove your finger at the end of each movement. Think of it as quickly flicking your finger up or down the screen. To choose your language, tap on the name of the language with your finger and release.

Figure 3.2 – Language Screen

3. You will now be asked to select which country or region you live in. Select your country or region by tapping down on the correct one using your finger and release. Again, you can scroll up and down by tapping down and moving your finger up or down and releasing to move throughout the list.

4. The next screen will ask you to choose your Wi-Fi network. It is best to setup your iPhone at home so you can connect to your home wireless network. After a few moments, a list of available networks will appear on your screen. Find your home network and tap on it with your finger. A new screen will appear asking for your wireless network password. Use the keyboard that appears at the bottom of your screen to tap in the password. Simply tap each letter or number one at a time to enter it in. You can use the "back arrow" key on the keyboard to backspace, and you can use the "123" key to see numbers and symbols. Also, to capitalize letters, you can use the shift key, which is the key with the upward arrow. Tapping on it will make the letters capital for ONE entry. Once you have entered your Wi-Fi password tap Join on your screen. (See Figure 3.3)

a. If you do not have Wi-Fi available near you, or are having trouble connecting to your Wi-Fi network, you can tap on <u>Use Mobile Connection</u> at the bottom of this screen.

Tap on the word Cancel to go back and select a different network.

Tap Join here or at the bottom when finished to join your Wi-Fi network.

Tap in this box to begin typing your network password.

This is the "Shift" key i.e. capitalize key.

Backspace key

This is the Symbols & Numbers key. Tap on this to bring up a keyboard with numbers and symbols such as !, ?, etc.

Figure 3.3 – Using the Keyboard and Wi-Fi Password

5. Now your iPhone will attempt to activate itself. This can take a few minutes. Once this is completed you will be brought to a new screen asking about Location Services.

6. It is recommended that you tap on <u>Enable Location Services</u> on this screen. Doing so will allow your iPhone to be used as a GPS. If you disable Location Services, you cannot use your iPhone as a GPS. You can always change your mind later.

7. On the next screen you will be asked to setup Touch ID if your iPhone is capable of it. Newer iPhones can use Touch ID. For now, tap on <u>Set up Touch ID later</u>.

8. Next, you will be asked to setup a passcode. A passcode is a 6-digit PIN that allows you to use your iPhone. You will need to remember this PIN, so I recommend writing it down somewhere safe. You will have to enter this PIN each time you restart your iPhone, and each time Touch ID fails to work properly. I CANNOT STRESS ENOUGH THAT YOU SHOULD WRITE DOWN AND REMEMBER THE PASSCODE YOU CREATE. IF YOU FORGET YOUR PASSCODE, THE PROCESS OF GETTING BACK INTO YOUR IPHONE IS DIFFICULT AND TIME CONSUMING. Once you've decided on a passcode, enter it in your

iPhone by tapping on the numbers. Once you have entered it the first time, you will be asked to confirm the passcode you created by entering it again. Do so and you will be brought to the next screen.

   a. If you prefer, you can use a 4-digit code or alphabetic code instead of a 6-digit passcode. To do this, tap on <u>Passcode options</u>. I will also show you later how to change your passcode.

9. Next you will be brought to the Apps & Data screen. Here you have to choose how to setup your iPhone.

   a. If this is your first iPhone, you will tap on <u>set up as new iPhone</u>. **Most Likely Option.

   b. If you have owned an iPhone before, and you want to migrate all your previous data to this new iPhone, and you know that previous data is backed up on iCloud, which is Apple's backup service, tap on <u>Restore from iCloud Backup</u>. You will then be asked to enter your Apple ID and password.

   c. If you have owned an iPhone before and you have that iPhone's data saved on iTunes on a computer, tap on <u>Restore from iTunes Backup</u>. You will then be told to plug your iPhone into your computer that has the iTunes backup installed.

   d. Lastly, if your previous phone was an Android phone and you want to migrate that data over, tap on <u>Move Data from Android</u> and follow the instructions on the screen. This option is a little more complicated and not recommended for new users.

10. Next, you will be brought to the Apple ID screen. THIS SCREEN AND THIS STEP IS VERY IMPORTANT. PLEASE FOLLOW THIS STEP VERY CAREFULLY. On this screen you are asked to login with your Apple ID. If you have ever owned an iPhone or iPad, chances are you have an Apple ID. Furthermore, if you currently use a Mac computer, you may have an Apple ID as well. This next sentence is very important. If you have other Apple devices and have an Apple ID, it is very important that you use the same Apple ID for all of your Apple devices. This way, all your purchases on one Apple ID will be available on all of your devices. Just to reiterate from earlier, an Apple ID is just an email address you have. If you know you already have an Apple ID, go to step 10A. If you do not have an Apple ID or are unsure, go to step 10B.

   a. If you already have an Apple ID from previous Apple devices, tap into the box to the right of the text "Apple ID" and enter your Apple ID email address. Remember, this is your email address that you have registered as an Apple ID with Apple. After you enter your email address, tap into the box next to password and type in your password using the keyboard that appears. When you are done, tap <u>Next</u> at the upper right.

   b. If you do not have an Apple ID, or this is your first Apple device, or you are not sure if you have an Apple ID, tap on the text at the bottom that says "<u>Don't have an Apple ID or forgot it?</u>"

i. On the next screen you can tap on "Forgot Apple ID or Password" if you think you have an Apple ID from a previous Apple device. If you don't have an Apple ID, tap on Create a Free Apple ID. **PLEASE NOTE, SETTING UP AN APPLE ID IS HIGHLY RECOMMENDED, AS YOU NEED AN APPLE ID TO DOWNLOAD APPS, BACKUP YOUR DEVICE, AND USE OTHER CRITICAL FEATURES.

1. First, you will be asked for your country or region. Select which country or region you live in by tapping on it with your finger. If this step doesn't appear, skip this step. Then tap Next.

2. On the next screen will be Apple's Terms and Conditions. Read through these at your leisure and tap on Agree, then Agree again to move on to the next screen.

3. Now you will have to enter in some information to create your Apple ID.

   a. In the email box, tap into the box next to email and type in the email address you want to use as your Apple ID. I suggest using your personal email address, one which you use often.

   b. Next you must create a password for your Apple ID. This box is NOT asking for your email password, it is simply asking you to create a password for your Apple ID. Tap into the password box and type in a password for your Apple ID. The password must contain at least 8 characters, and it must contain at least 1 capital letter, 1 lower case letter, and at least 1 number.

   c. Now tap into the verify box and type in your new password again to verify it is the same. REMEMBER THIS PASSWORD. WRITE IT DOWN SOMEWHERE SAFE IF YOU MUST, BUT YOU WILL NEED THIS PASSWORD LATER.

   d. You may need to scroll down on your iPhone to reach the next information. Remember, to scroll, tap down on the screen with your finger and then move your finger up or down on the scroll and release your finger at the end.

   e. Now you must choose security questions. These questions are used in case you ever forget your password and you need to get into your Apple ID account. You will have to select 3 security questions and answer them. Tap into each security question box to select which security question you want to use. To choose a security question, tap on the corresponding text of the question you want to use. After you have selected a question, you will then automatically be brought into the next box where you can type in the answer to your question. Type in the answer to the specify question in this box, then tap on <u>Go/Return</u> on the keyboard to move on to the next question. Repeat this step for the 3 security questions.

    f. Now you need to enter a rescue email if you have one. A rescue email is another email address you have access to in case you forget your password to your Apple ID and/or you lose access to your primary email address. So if you have an additional email address, I suggest entering it into here.

    g. Next you will have to enter in your date of birth. This is required because some apps have an age requirement. Tap into each box for month, day, and year, and use your finger to select the appropriate value. You can scroll through these values the same as always, by tapping down on the screen and moving your finger up and down.

4. When all this information is entered. Tap on the words <u>Next</u>.

5. Now you will have to enter your billing information. Your billing information is required in case you ever decide to purchase a "paid app" or make purchases from within an app. You will not be charged anything here when you enter your billing information.

    a. Select your type of credit card (Visa, MC, Discover, etc.).

    b. Enter in your billing address by tapping into each box and typing it in.

    c. Enter your phone number into the phone number box.

6. Tap <u>Next</u>.

7. The next screen will ask you to verify your account. All this means is an email message was sent to the email you chose to use as your Apple ID. When you have time, check your email and open the link that was sent to you by clicking on it. This will verify your account. You do not have to do this now, but it should be done before starting Chapter 3.5. For now, tap <u>Done</u> on this screen.

8. Your Apple ID has been successfully created! Occasionally, you will be asked on your iPhone to enter your Apple ID password. When a popup box appears asking for this password, just enter it in on your keyboard. Remember to use correct capitalization.

11. The long creation of your Apple ID is over. Now you may be brought to another Terms and Conditions page. On this page, read through the terms and scroll down to the very bottom of the document. Remember, to scroll, tap down on the screen and swipe your

finger up and down and release. Once you've reached the bottom of the terms and conditions tap on <u>Agree</u>. Then tap on <u>Agree</u> again.

12. The next screen will be the Siri screen. On this screen you will be asked whether you want to setup Siri. I recommend you set it up now, so tap on <u>Setup Siri</u>. You will be asked to speak into your iPhone a few words. Follow the directions that appear on your screen. You will have to speak about 5 phrases. All this does is train Siri to recognize your voice. Siri is just Apple's artificial helper, which listens to you and follows your command. Once this step is complete, your iPhone will read "Hey Siri is Ready," and you can tap on <u>Continue</u>. If you are having trouble setting up Siri, just tap on <u>Set Up Siri Later</u> at the bottom of your screen.

13. The next screen will be the diagnostics screen, which is basically asking you whether you want your iPhone to periodically send data to Apple to help Apple fix bugs and glitches. This is completely up to you if you want to enable this or not. Tap on <u>Send to Apple</u> or <u>Don't Send</u> to continue.

14. Next a screen with "App Analytics" may appear. This is similar to the previous step. Tap on <u>Share</u> or <u>Don't Share</u>.

15. If you have an iPhone 7 or newer, the next screen will be the "Meet the New Home Button" screen. If this screen appears for you, follow the 15a and 15b steps, otherwise skip to step 16.
    a. Tap on <u>Get Started</u>
    b. Follow the directions on the screen. Your iPhone is merely asking you which haptic you want to feel when you press on the home button. To do this: tap on a number on your screen, then press the <u>home button</u> to see how it feels. Try this for the numbers 1, 2, and 3, and once you have found the feel you like, tap on <u>Next</u> at the upper right.

16. The next screen will be the Display Zoom screen. All this is asking is whether you want a zoomed-in display or normal display. A zoomed-in display is optimal for people with vision problems. Tap on <u>Choose a view</u>, then using the two tabs at the top, check out the different views for Standard and Zoomed by tapping on <u>Standard</u> and then <u>Zoomed</u>. When you found the one you prefer, tap on <u>Next</u> at the upper right.

17. You are all done! Your iPhone is officially set up and ready to use. Tap on <u>Get Started</u> on the next screen to finish the setup and start using your iPhone.

After you have completed the initial setup you will be brought to your home screen. Remember, your home screen is the screen that shows all your apps.

Chapter 3.5 – Update your iOS Now

Before we begin Chapter 4, it's important that you check to see if an update is available to your iPhone's software, otherwise known as iOS. In order to do this, follow these steps:

1. On your home screen, which shows all of your apps, there should be an app called Settings. Tap on the app with your finger to open it. (Figure 3.5.1)

Figure 3.5.1 – Settings App on Home Screen

2. Next, tap on the word General, which you should see somewhere on your screen. You can scroll up and down if you cannot find it.

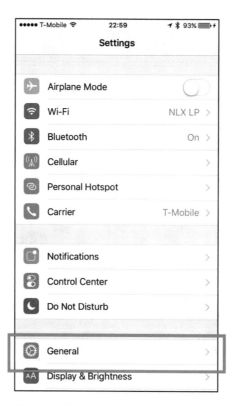

Figure 3.5.2 – Settings -> General

3. Next, tap on Software Update.

4. Your iPhone will check to see if there is an update available. If there is an update available, your iPhone will say so, and there will be an option to Download/Install. If this option appears, tap on Download and Install or Install. If there is not an update available, your iPhone will say iOS X.y.z, where the X, y, and z will be numbers. For the sake of this book, the only number that matters is the first number. So for this book, you will want that first number to be 11 or greater if you have an iPhone 6, 6s, 7, 8, or SE. If you have an iPhone 5, 5s, or 5c, then you will want that first number to be 10 or greater. It will also say your Software is Up to Date.

5. If an update is available, install the update by tapping on Install or Download and Install. Your iPhone will download and install the software update. This could take some time, and you will need to be connected to Wi-Fi to download the update. (See Chapter 4 to learn how to connect to Wi-Fi if you have not done so in the initial setup). Let the update install, and your iPhone will restart when it is finished, and then you are ready to continue. If your iOS software is already up to date, you are ready to continue.

6. You can press the home button on your iPhone to return to the home screen.

If a software update is available for your iPhone, it is HIGHLY recommended that you update it.

Chapter 4 – Navigating your iPhone

All you need to use your iPhone are your fingers. Everything is based on the touch screen and the home button on your iPhone. Here at the home screen (Figure 4.1), which is just the screen that shows you all of your apps, you can open an app, which is a program on your phone that can do tasks and enable features, by lightly touching down on the square with your finger and releasing quickly. To then leave the app and return to the home screen, press down on the home button.

Your home screen is actually made up of multiple screens, to accommodate however many apps you have on your iPhone. To move through different pages of apps on your iPhone's home screen, touch down on the screen with one of your fingers, and then drag your finger to the left or the right, like you would be dragging a page, then release. If at any time you need to return back to the main home screen, just push down on the home button.

Tap on an App to open it.

Tap and swipe down on your home screen to bring up Search

Tap and swipe your finger left and right to switch between different home screens

Figure 4.1 – The Home Screen

Search your iPhone

You can search your iPhone for anything using the Search function. To use this function, touch down somewhere on your home screen, and drag your finger down then release. (Figure 4.1) This is a great way to search for apps on your iPhone when you have too many to remember them all. To get back to the home screen simply press the <u>home button</u> again, or swipe up with your finger.

Today Screen

You may have noticed, that when you are on your main home screen and you swipe your finger to the right that you are brought to what is called the "Today" screen. (Figure 4.2) This screen shows you if you have anything coming up on your calendar, along with some suggestions for apps that you use. There may also be more information on this screen such as your local weather. You can tap on anything here to explore it more. To get back to the home screen press the <u>home button</u> or swipe to the left with your finger.

<u>Figure 4.2</u> – The Today Screen

Connecting to Wi-Fi

Connecting to Wi-Fi is one of the most important things you should do with your iPhone. When you are connected to Wi-Fi, your internet speeds are generally faster, and you are not using valuable cellular data. You may have connected to your home wireless network when you first set up your iPhone, in which case you are already good to go. You can tell if you are connected to Wi-Fi by looking for the Wi-Fi symbol at the top left of your screen. If the Wi-Fi symbol appears, it means you are connected to Wi-Fi. (Figure 4.3) Once you have connected to a Wi-Fi network, your iPhone will remember that network, and you will not need to ever manually connect to it again. Each time your iPhone comes in range of that network it will connect automatically.

To connect to a Wi-Fi network, follow these steps:

1. Open the Settings app on your home screen by tapping down on it and quickly releasing.
2. Tap Wi-Fi
3. Your iPhone will search for networks. If you are already connected to a network, it will appear directly under the words Wi-Fi and a checkmark will be next to its name. Look at the network names under where it says "CHOOSE A NETWORK…" When you see the network you want to connect to, tap on it with your finger.
4. You will then have to enter your Wi-Fi password. Enter this password using the keyboard, and then tap on Join at the upper right. (For more on using the iPhone keyboard, see Figure 3.3 in Chapter 3).
5. Your iPhone will join the Wi-Fi network as long as the password was entered correctly. Remember, Wi-Fi passwords are case sensitive. Once you have joined a Wi-Fi network, you will never have to manually join that network again, as your iPhone will connect to it automatically from now on.
6. Press the home button to return to the home screen.

TIP: If you do not know your home wireless network name and password, it may be located on the back or bottom of your wireless router. Check the back of your router to see if that information is there.

When you see this Wi-Fi symbol, it means you are currently connected to a Wi-Fi network.

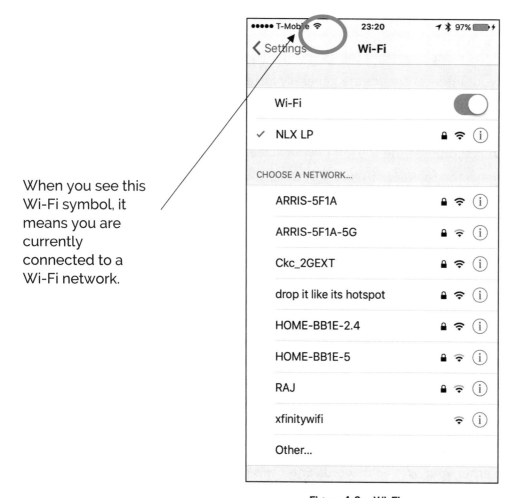

Figure 4.3 – Wi-Fi

Chapter 5 – Apple ID

I have already discussed the concept of your Apple ID throughout this text, but it is worth emphasizing some more. The most common questions I receive about using iPhones are related to Apple IDs. So in this chapter, I will cover everything you need to know about your Apple ID.

Important

How to Check Your Apple ID

If you created an Apple ID during the initial setup of your iPhone, great! If you did, please write down your Apple ID email and password somewhere safe. You will need that information from time to time. If you haven't created an Apple ID or are not sure, there is a way to check. Follow these steps:

1. Open the Settings app on your iPhone by tapping on Settings on your home screen.
2. Scroll down through Settings until you find iTunes & App Store and then tap on it.
3. On this screen, at the top, will be a box labeled Apple ID: and inside this box will be your Apple ID if you have created one and are signed in. There should be an email address in there. If there isn't an email address in there, it will read "Sign In" instead. (See Figure 5.1)

Now you know whether you are signed in to your iPhone with an Apple ID, and what that Apple ID is. If you are signed in, write down and remember your Apple ID. If you are not signed in, and do not have an Apple ID, you need to create one now.

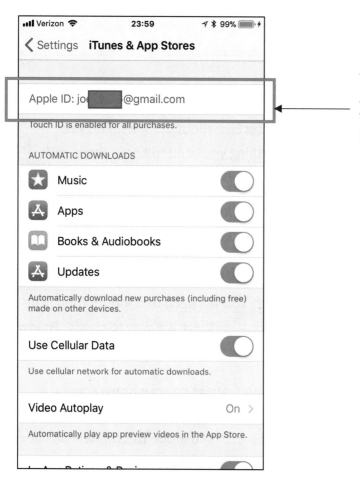

This box here will show your Apple ID. If you are not signed in with your Apple ID, it will say Sign In, which you can tap on.

Figure 5.1 – Settings -> iTunes & App Store

How to Create an Apple ID

If you do not have an Apple ID, you need to create one. Simply put, you need an Apple ID to use many of the functions available on your iPhone. To create an Apple ID, follow these steps:

1. Go to your home screen. (Remember, you can get to your home screen at any time by pressing the home button once.)

2. Find the app called iTunes Store and tap on it to open it.

3. When the app loads completely, scroll down to the very bottom and tap Sign In.

4. If you have an Apple ID, sign in with your Apple ID login credentials by tapping on Use Existing Apple ID. If you do not have one, tap on Create New Apple ID.

5. Follow the steps in Chapter 3, First-time Setup, step 10b.

*Alternatively, you can create an Apple ID from a computer by visiting
https://appleid.apple.com/account

Signing in with Your Apple ID

If you have created your Apple ID on your iPhone, you will most likely be signed in automatically on your iPhone. Your Apple ID is used for many apps, and it may be necessary to sign in to all of these apps with your Apple ID. Follow these steps to sign in to your iPhone with your Apple ID:

1. On your home screen open the Settings app.
2. Scroll down to iTunes and App Store and tap it.
3. Tap the Apple ID box at the top and tap Sign In. If your Apple ID already appears, you are already signed in.
4. Enter in your Apple ID email address and password and sign in.
5. Once signed in, tap the back arrow at the upper left where it says Settings.
6. Now tap on the big box at the very top where it says Apple ID or your name. (Figure 5.2)
7. At the top will be your name and email address if you are already signed in to your Apple ID for iCloud. If your name does not appear, tap on Sign In.
8. Enter your Apple ID email address and password and tap Sign In.
9. Use the back arrows again at the upper left to return to the main Settings page.
10. Now we want to check and make sure your Apple ID is signed in for all Apple services.
11. Find in Settings the Messages box and tap it.
12. Now tap where it says Send & Receive. (Figure 5.3)
13. At the top where it says Apple ID, make sure your Apple ID appears there. If it does not, tap on it and sign in.
14. Use the back arrows at the upper left to return to the main Settings page, and tap on FaceTime.
15. In the Apple ID box, make sure your Apple ID appears. If it does not appear, tap on the box and sign in with your Apple ID.
16. Press the home button to return the home screen.

You should now be signed in completely with your Apple ID.

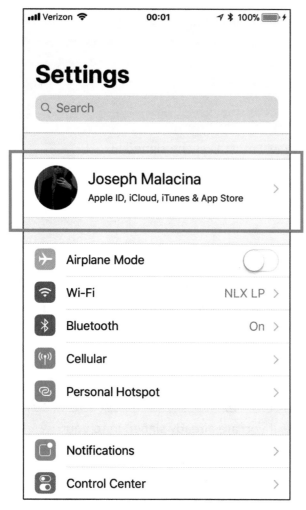

Figure 5.2 – Settings -> Big Box at Top (Apple ID)

Figure 5.3 – Settings -> Messages -> Send & Receive

How to Use Your Apple ID

Now that you are all signed in with your Apple ID, how can you use it? You do not really need to worry about that actually. You will be using your Apple ID automatically. Every time you download an app you will be using your Apple ID. Occasionally, your iPhone may show a popup box asking you for your Apple ID password. When this appears, just enter your password and tap OK/Sign In. Your iPhone will ask for its password periodically for security purposes. Make sure you remember this password!

All the confusing stuff is now out of the way. Once you are signed in with your Apple ID, you do not need to worry about it anymore as long as you remember your Apple ID password. It is finally time to get into actually using the iPhone.

Chapter 6 – Your Contact List

Your contact list is an essential tool on your iPhone. With it, you can store your contacts' phone numbers, email addresses, and other vital data.

Importing Contacts

When you first get your new iPhone, you may want to transfer the contacts from your previous cell phone to your iPhone. The best way to do this is to have your wireless provider do it for you. Most wireless provider stores can transfer and import your contacts using their own equipment. Unfortunately, for some cell phones you will not be able to do this, in which case you will have to create your contacts manually.

If you have had an iPhone in the past, your contacts will transfer automatically when you sign in with the same Apple ID. The same goes for Macs. If you created a contact list on a Mac computer, when you sign in with your Apple ID on your iPhone those same contacts will be automatically imported. You can also import your Outlook contacts to your iPhone using iTunes software. This is much more complicated, and can be learned by visiting www.infinityguides.com and searching for "iTunes".

Creating Contacts

Let us see how we can create a contact. Here are the steps: (See Figures 6.1 & 6.2)

1. Open the Phone app from your home screen.
2. At the bottom, tap on the tab that says Contacts. (Figure 6.1)
3. At the upper right of your screen, there will be a + sign. Tap on the + sign. (Figure 6.1)
4. You will now be brought to a screen where you can create a contact.
5. Tap into each corresponding box to type in an entry for the new contact. You can enter in their First name, Last name, and Company.
6. Tap into the add phone box to add their phone number.
7. Tap into the add email box to add their email, if applicable.
8. By scrolling down further, you can choose to enter in additional information including their home address, birthday, and other information.

9. You can also choose a specific ringtone for a contact.

10. Once you have added all the information you want for your new contact, tap <u>Done</u> at the upper right.

11. Your new contact has just been created.

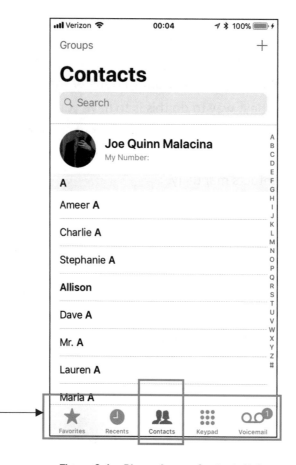

These icons at the bottom are called *tabs.* Tap on the <u>Contacts</u> tab to open the Contacts screen.

<u>Figure 6.1</u> – Phone App -> Contacts Tab

Tapping on add photo will allow you to set a picture for your contact that is saved in your Photos app.

When done tap here.

You can tap into each box to type in contact information.

Tap the green + icon to add the corresponding information such as a phone number or email address.

You can scroll (tap down on screen and swipe finger up/down) to enter more information for your contact.

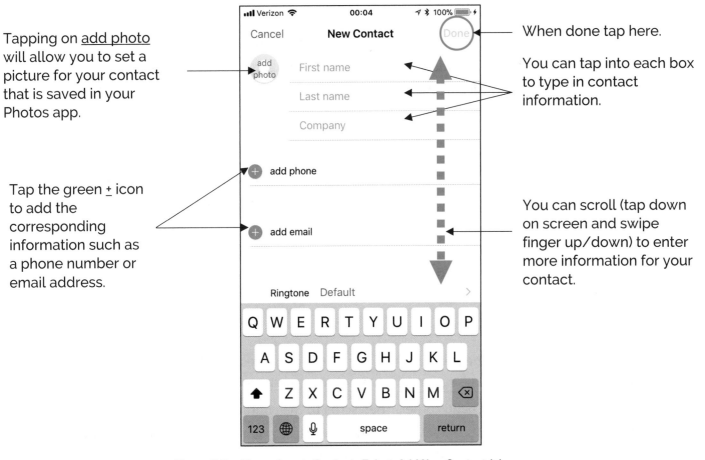

Figure 6.2 – Phone App -> Contacts Tab -> Add New Contact (+)

Browsing Contacts

At any time, you can view your contact list by opening the Phone app and tapping the Contacts tab at the bottom. Now you will see a list of all of your contacts. You can browse through this list by simply tapping down on the screen and scrolling up or down.

TIP: To quickly browse through your contacts by their last name. Tap down and scroll on the letters at the far right of your screen.

You can also tap into the search bar at the top of your Contacts screen to search for a contact directly.

To view a contact's information, simply tap on their name.

Editing or Deleting a Contact

To edit a contact, tap on their _name_ inside the contact list, and then tap edit at the upper right. Now you can edit all of their information. To delete a certain aspect of their information, simply tap on the red minus sign next to it. When you are done editing a contact tap on Done at the upper right.

To delete a contact, tap on their _name_ inside the contact list. Now tap edit at the upper right. Now scroll down all the way to the bottom of the contact's information, and tap on Delete Contact. A confirmation will appear, where you can tap on Delete Contact again to confirm the deletion.

Favorites List
(Figure 6.3)

The favorites list is basically the speed dial of your iPhone. To access you Favorites List, open the Phone app, and then tap the Favorites tab. To add a contact to your Favorites List, first tap the plus sign in the upper left hand corner. Then scroll to the contact you wish to add to your favorites, and then tap on that contact. Now tap on which segment of that contact you want to be on your favorites list, such as text message or phone call. Your contact will now appear in your favorites list.

Tap the ± symbol to add a contact to your Favorites list.

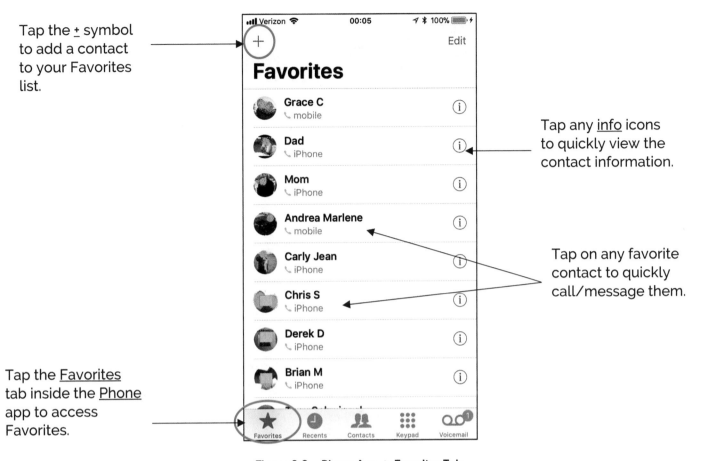

Tap any <u>info</u> icons to quickly view the contact information.

Tap on any favorite contact to quickly call/message them.

Tap the <u>Favorites</u> tab inside the <u>Phone</u> app to access Favorites.

<u>Figure 6.3</u> – Phone App -> Favorites Tab

Chapter 7 – Phone Calls

At its heart the iPhone is a great cell phone. Making and receiving calls is easy and user-friendly, and we will explore that in this chapter.

Making a Call

There are numerous ways to make a call using your iPhone. I will cover some of the most basic ways.

How to Dial a Call (Figure 7.1)

1. Open the <u>Phone</u> app on your home screen
2. Tap the <u>Keypad</u> tab at the bottom
3. Tap in the <u>number</u> you wish to call, one digit at a time
4. Tap the <u>green phone icon</u> to start the call

Tap in the phone number using the digits on your screen.

After tapping in the phone number, tap the <u>green call icon</u> to initiate the call.

Figure 7.1 – Phone App -> Keypad Tab

How to Call Someone on Your Contact List (Figure 7.2)

1. Open the Phone app
2. Tap the Contacts tab
3. Find the contact you wish to call and tap on their *name* to view their contact details.
4. Now, to start the call you can either tap the call icon inside the contact's information or tap on the corresponding phone number within the contact to start the call.

Tap on any of the blue icons to initiate the action (i.e. a phone call, text message, email, etc.)

You can also tap directly on their contact information to start a call, email, or text message.

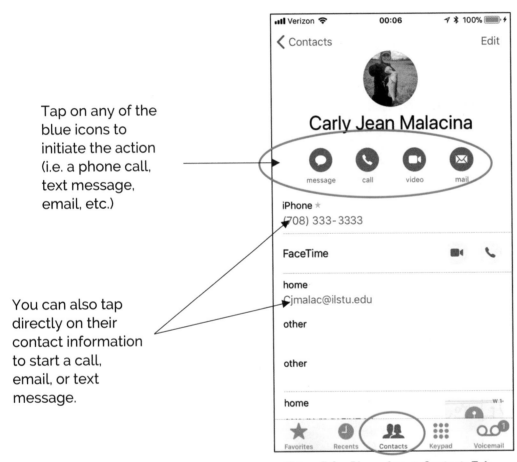

Figure 7.2 – Phone App -> Contacts Tab

How to Call Someone on Your Favorites List (See Figure 6.3)

1. Open the Phone app
2. Tap the Favorites tab
3. Tap on the *contact* in your Favorites List that has a small phone icon underneath their name to immediately start a call with them

Receiving a Call

When you receive a call, a screen will appear (See Figure 7.3). If your iPhone is currently unlocked (i.e. your iPhone screen is on), all you need to do to answer the call is tap on the green phone icon. When you do, you will now be connected to the call.

Figure 7.3 – Receiving a Call, iPhone Unlocked

When you receive a call when your iPhone is currently locked, you will notice a slider appearing at the bottom of your screen. (See Figure 7.4). To answer the call, touch down on the green phone icon, and slide it to the right with your finger, releasing at the end. This will connect you to the call.

To answer the call, tap down on the green phone icon and slide your finger to the right, releasing at the end

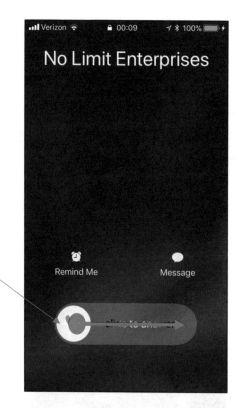

Figure 7.4 – Receiving a Call, iPhone Locked

You can always reject a call by pressing the power button on your iPhone when a call is incoming.

Call Functions

During a phone call, you have several functions available to you. Looking at your screen during a call (Figure 7.5), there are several buttons on your screen. They do the following if you tap on them:

- **Mute –** Mutes your side of the call. In other words, the person you are talking to on the phone will not be able to hear anything from your side until you touch mute again and turn mute off.
- **Keypad –** Brings up a touch-tone keypad, in case you need to work through a touch-tone system.
- **Speaker –** Tapping speaker turns on speakerphone. Tap it again to turn it off.
- **Add Call –** Tapping on add call lets you add another person to the call, such as 3-way calling. (If part of your service).

- **FaceTime –** FaceTime lets you connect to the person you are talking to over a FaceTime call, which is a video call. This only works when you are talking to someone who has a FaceTime enabled device. (More on FaceTime later in this book).
- **Contacts –** Tapping on <u>contacts</u> will bring you to your contact list.

You can also browse through your iPhone while on a call by simply pressing on the <u>home button</u>. To get back to the call screen itself mid-call, tap on the <u>green bar</u> at the top of your screen.

Figure 7.5 – In-Call Options

Recent Calls

To access your recent calls list, open the <u>Phone</u> app and touch the <u>Recents</u> tab at the bottom. This screen lists all your recent calls. For names listed in red, these are missed calls. The times indicated on the right are the times the call took place. To quickly call someone on your recent calls list, simply tap down on their *name* and your iPhone will call them. You can also view more information about a recent call by tapping on the <u>information circle</u> to the right.

Voicemail

(See Figure 7.6)

A common question I get is how to setup voicemail on the iPhone. Unfortunately, there is no easy answer. The reason is because voicemail is completely controlled by your cellular provider. You will have to contact them to set it up.

For some providers, you can setup voicemail from the Phone app. Just open the Phone app, tap on Voicemail at the bottom right, and your voicemails will be listed. You can tap on one to listen to a it. You can also set your voicemail greeting by tapping on Greeting at the upper left. Again, this setup won't work for everyone, as it is completely controlled by your cellular provider. Your best bet is to contact them in order to set your voicemail up.

Tap to set voicemail greeting (if applicable).

Tap to manage voicemails (delete).

Tap to listen to that specific voicemail (if applicable).

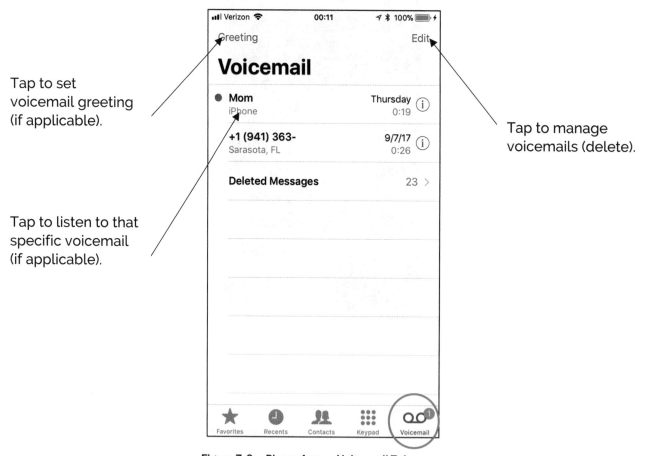

Figure 7.6 – Phone App -> Voicemail Tab

Chapter 8 – Text Messaging

The iPhone is a wonderful tool for text messaging. The ease in which to send and receive text messages is astounding, and the way in which texts are organized is even better. Let's explore the Messages app.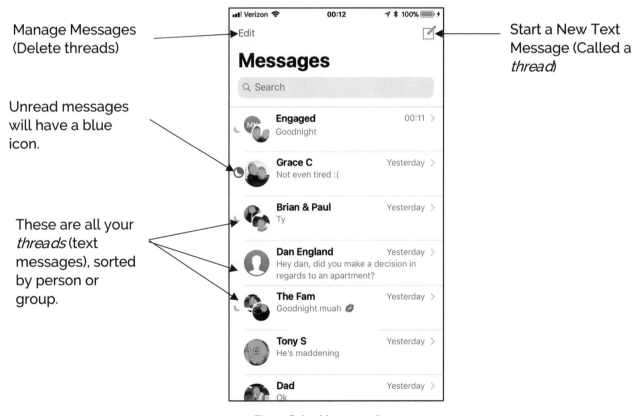

Somewhere on your home screen will be the <u>Messages</u> app. Tap on it to open it up. This is where all of your text messaging will take place, and where all of your text messages will be stored.

Before we dive in, let me explain some texting jargon. When you exchange a text message with someone, it is generally called a conversation or thread. In this book, we will call any text conversation with someone or a group of people a "thread." (<u>Figure 8.1</u>)

Manage Messages
(Delete threads)

Start a New Text
Message (Called a
thread)

Unread messages
will have a blue
icon.

These are all your
threads (text
messages), sorted
by person or
group.

Figure 8.1 – Messages App

Sending a Text Message

To send your first text message on your iPhone, first tap the <u>Square and Pencil</u> icon at the upper right of your screen. (Figure 8.1) This will start a new text thread. In the screen that appears, you can type in the name of one your contacts and as you are typing, your iPhone will make suggestions as to whom you are trying to text. Once you see their name, you can tap on their *name* to complete the entry. (Figure 8.2)

Alternatively, you can use your keyboard to type in the exact phone number of someone you want to text.

Next you can tap into the Message bar or iMessage bar near the middle of your screen. Now you can use your keypad to type in a message. Once that message is ready to be sent, tap the up arrow icon to send the message. (Figure 8.2)

Search your contact list for a recipient to add to thread.

Tap in here to enter recipient via contact name or phone number or Apple ID.

Tap in this space, called the Message or iMessage bar, to begin typing in a message.

Tap to send when message is entered. Blue = iMessage. Green = Text Message

Figure 8.2 – Messages App -> Start New Thread (Pencil & Square Icon)

Receiving a Message

When you receive a message, it will appear in the Messages app. (See Figure 8.1). Unread messages will have a blue icon next to the thread. To view the message, open the thread by tapping on the <u>thread's *name*</u>. Your entire text message conversation will now be shown, including any new messages that you have received from this thread. You can scroll up and down through the history of the conversation using your finger. At any time while inside a thread, you can return to the main Messages screen by tapping on the <u>back arrow</u> at the upper left.

Group Threads

Text messaging is not reserved for a single person. You can create group threads where multiple people can exchange text messages. The process is exactly the same:

1. Tap the <u>square and pencil icon</u> at the upper right to create a new message.
2. Enter in the name of a person you want to text, of the group. Tap on their <u>*name*</u> once it appears in suggestions.
3. Now type in another name of a person you also want to be a part of the group thread, and tap on their <u>*name*</u> in suggestions when it appears.
4. Add as many people to the thread as you wish.
5. When ready to start conversing, tap into the <u>Message box</u> and begin typing away.

This group thread will now be saved in your Messages app and you can converse in there any time you wish.

iMessage

(See <u>Figure 8.3</u>)

iMessage is a special term used for text messages exchanged between people who use Apple devices. For instance, you may notice when texting certain people that your messages will appear as the color blue. Conversely, you will notice when texting other people that your messages will appear as the color green. (<u>Figure 8.4</u>) When they appear blue, that means you are sending iMessages to each other. In other words, you both are using Apple devices such as an iPhone, iPad, or Mac to send your text messages. iMessages (blue) are different because they are not sent as cellular text messages. In other words, they do not count against your text message count if your cellular plan limits them. Also, when you are conversing with someone using iMessage, there are additional options available to you, which we will now cover.

Figure 8.3 – iMessage Example

Figure 8.4 – Regular Text Message

Special Effects

(See Figure 8.5)

There are a ton of special effects and add-ons you can use with the Messages app. For instance, if you want to text message a picture to someone, tap the camera icon to the left of the message bar. Now you can browse through your saved photos on the bottom by swiping left and right, and you can send one of those photos by tapping on it and then tapping the send icon. Alternatively, you can take a picture to send by swiping to the left and tapping on Camera. (Figure 8.6)

There are more effects you can send as well. We will not cover all of them in here, but you can send emoticons by tapping on the smiley face in your keyboard. More effects are available by tapping on the App Store icon. Lastly, you can send voice messages to the thread by using the microphone to the right of the message bar. Take the time to play around with these features at your leisure to see all you can do with Messages. You will notice that some features can only be used when exchanging iMessages with another Apple user.

See thread details including who is in thread

This is the *back arrow*, it will always bring you back one screen. (Used in many apps)

Name of thread or contact name

Send Photos

Send audio messages

See apps for Messages

Send emoticons

Figure 8.5 – Messages Features including Special Effects

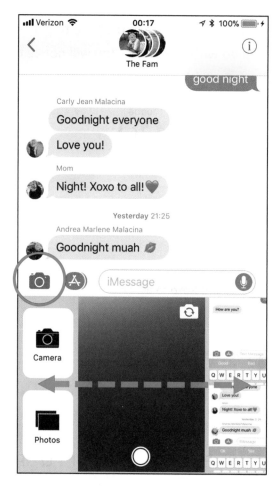

Figure 8.6 – Sending a Photo through Messages app

Managing Messages

An important aspect of messages is managing them. Let's take a look at a couple key management features that are prudent to know.

How to Delete Threads

You can delete an entire thread by following these steps:

1. Open the Messages app.
2. Tap Edit at the upper left
3. Tap each thread you want to delete, until they are check-marked.
4. Tap Delete at the lower right.

How to Delete Individual Texts

1. Open a thread in the Messages app.

2. Find the exact text you want to delete, and tap and hold on it until some options appear. (Figure 8.7)

3. Tap More at the bottom.

4. Now you can tap each individual text within a thread to be check-marked that you want deleted.

5. Tap the trash icon at the lower left to delete the selected texts.

Tap and hold with your finger on an individual text in order to bring up these options. Then tap on More... to select texts for deletion.

You can emote a text by using these icons, similar to "liking" a text. (iMessage only)

Figure 8.7 – Managing Individual Text Messages

Thread Details

Thread details offer a glimpse into certain information about a thread, such as who is in the thread, and any pictures exchanged in the thread. To access thread information, simply open a thread in Messages, and then tap the information icon at the upper right.

Chapter 9 – Email

Your iPhone has the ability to seamlessly manage your email accounts. It is quite convenient when you can quickly reply to an email in 10 seconds straight from your iPhone. All of your emails and email accounts are located within the Mail app, which we will get to shortly. For now, let's start by adding your existing email account to your iPhone.

Adding an Email Address to iPhone

1. Open the Settings app.
2. Find the Accounts & Passwords tab, and tap on it. (For iOS 10, tap on Mail tab, then Accounts)
3. Tap Add Account.
4. Look through the list of pre-populated email accounts such as AOL, Google (Gmail), and Yahoo. If you have one of these accounts, tap on it. If your account does not appear, tap on Other. (Figure 9.1)
5. If you tapped on a pre-populated account, follow the instructions that appear on your screen. Most likely you will just have to enter in your email address and password. If you tapped on Other, tap on Add Mail Account. (Figure 9.2)
6. Now type in the requested information. When done, tap Next at the upper right. (Figure 9.3)
7. Your iPhone will attempt to add your email given the information you provided. For most email accounts, this should work with no issues. However, for less common email accounts, your iPhone may require more information such as incoming and outgoing server addresses. If this is the case for you, you will have to contact your email provider in order to get this information.
8. Continue following the instructions that appear on your screen until you have reached the end. You can continue by tapping on Next/Done at the upper right.

Once your email account has successfully been added, you are ready to use email on your iPhone. You can add multiple email addresses to your iPhone if you wish.

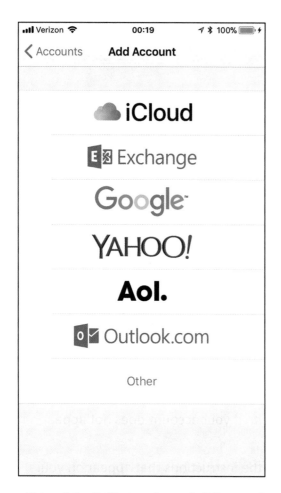

Figure 9.1 – Settings -> Accounts & Passwords ->
Add Account

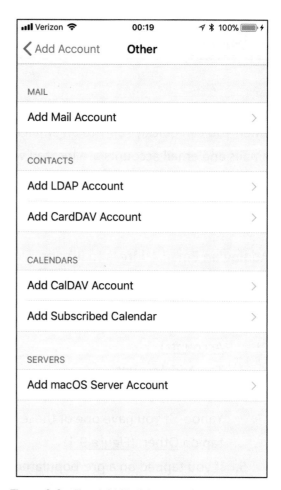

Figure 9.2 – Tap Add Mail Account for standard
email addresses, if you chose Other.

Tap Next when all
fields are filled in

Fill in these boxes and
be sure to include the
email address and email
address password that
you want to add to your
iPhone. The description
may fill in automatically.

Figure 9.3 – Enter your Email Address Information Here

Checking Your Email

To check your email, we need to use the Mail app, which is located somewhere on your home

screen. Tap on it to open it up.

Your email accounts will now be listed. You can use the back arrow at the upper left to view all
of your email accounts. Simply tap on an account to view your email for that specific account.

Viewing Email

To view an email, simply tap on it and it will appear full screen. (Figure 9.4) From here you
have several options available to you (Figure 9.5). Looking at the icons at the bottom of your
screen, they perform the following by tapping on them.

- **Flag –** Flags or marks the message.

- **Folder** – Moves the message to a different folder.
- **Trash** – Deletes or Archives the message.
- **Arrow** – Replies, forwards, or prints the email.
- **Square with Pencil** – Creates a new email.

You can use the <u>back arrow</u> at the upper left to go back.

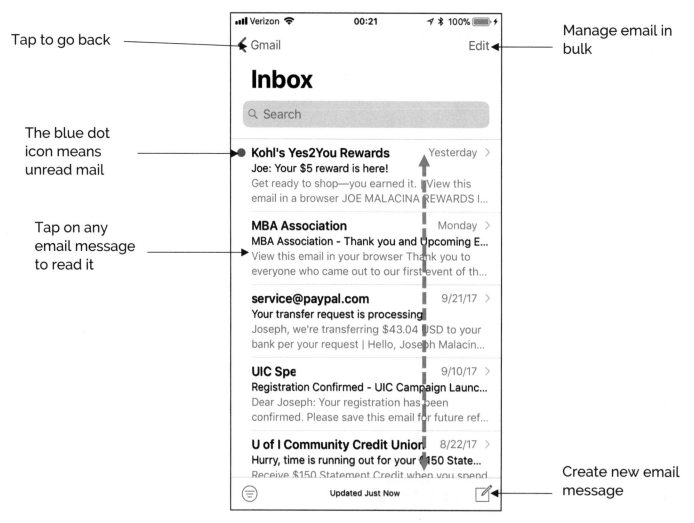

Tap to go back

Manage email in bulk

The blue dot icon means unread mail

Tap on any email message to read it

Create new email message

<u>Figure 9.4 – The Mail App</u>

Tap to go back ⎯⎯⎯⎯⎯

Tap to quickly view next or previous email

Email controls ⎯⎯⎯⎯⎯

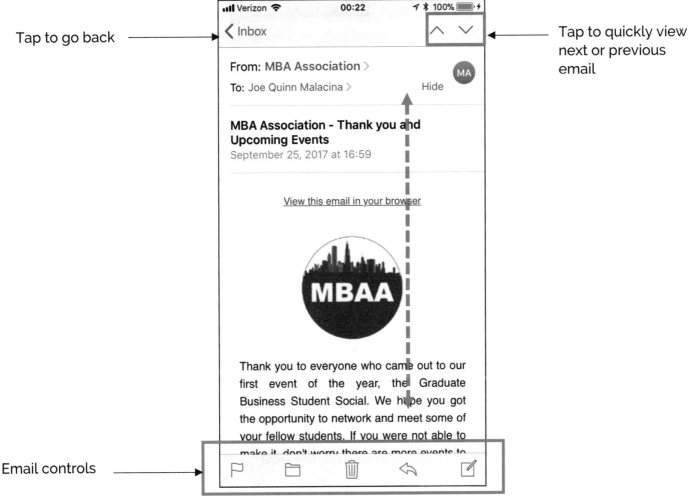

Figure 9.5 – Viewing an Email

Sending Email

See (Figure 9.6)

At any time from the Mail app, you can create a new email by tapping the square and pencil icon at the lower right. This will bring up a new message box. Full steps are:

1. Tap the square and pencil icon at the lower right inside the Mail app.
2. Enter in the email address or contact name of the intended recipient. Use the + icon to search through your contacts.
3. Tap into the subject line, and type in the subject.
4. Tap into the message body, and type in the email message.
5. Tap Send at the upper right, or tap Cancel at the upper left to cancel the message.

Enter recipient email address

Enter email subject

Enter email message

Tap to send

Tap to search your contact list

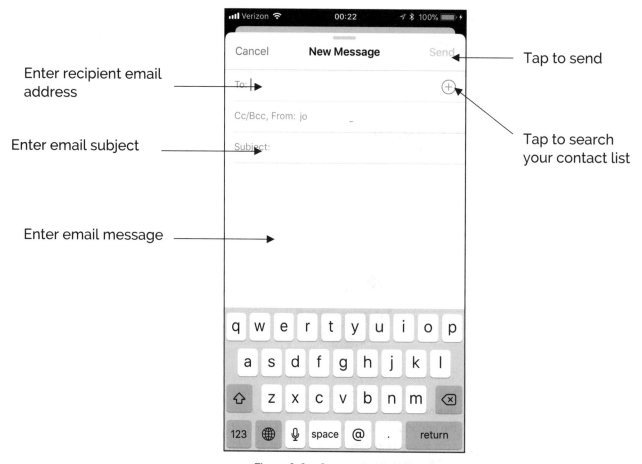

Figure 9.6 – Composing New Email

Managing Email

To Delete Email(s)

1. Tap an email account or folder to view all emails in that category.
2. Tap <u>Edit</u> at the upper right.
3. Tap each email you want to manage.
4. Use the text at the bottom to manage. Tap on <u>Mark</u>, <u>Move</u>, or <u>Archive/Delete</u>.
5. To cancel, tap <u>Cancel</u> at the upper right.

You can quickly delete an individual email by tapping on its preview, then swiping to the left.

Chapter 10 – Web Browsing

One of the signature features of the iPhone is the ease in which you can surf the web. To access the Internet, open the <u>Safari app</u> on your home screen.   Safari is where you will be doing all of your internet browsing, unless you download a different app for web browsing.

Visiting Web Pages

Safari is Apple's web browser optimized for the iPhone. In Safari, you can visit web pages as well as search the web using your favorite search engine. By default, Google is set as the current search engine. To search the web, tap in the box at the top of the screen and type in your search parameters, then touch <u>GO</u> on your keypad. If you want to visit a webpage directly, touch in the same box and type in the web address, followed by tapping <u>GO</u>. (<u>Figure 10.1</u>)

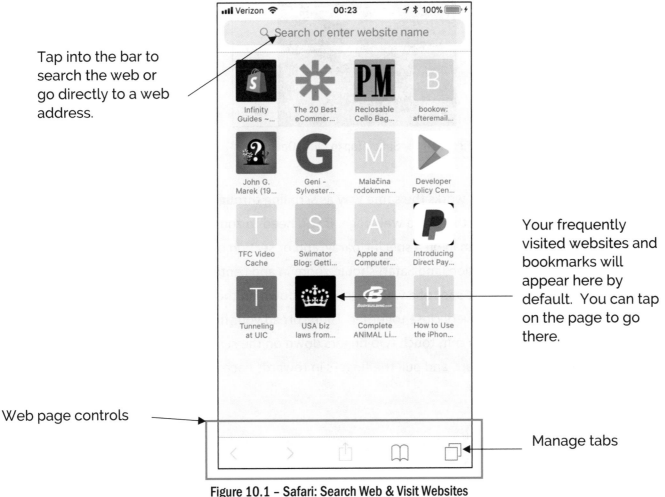

Tap into the bar to search the web or go directly to a web address.

Your frequently visited websites and bookmarks will appear here by default. You can tap on the page to go there.

Web page controls

Manage tabs

<u>Figure 10.1</u> – Safari: Search Web & Visit Websites

Navigating the web on the iPhone is a unique experience and takes some practice. Think of your finger as the mouse pointer, and touching down on the screen as a click. To open a link, simply touch down on it with your finger. (Figure 10.2)

Tap on the page to perform a classical *click of the mouse.* Do this to open links and pages.

Figure 10.2 – Safari: Tap to Click (Open Pages)

Scrolling through web pages works the same way as scrolling through apps. Simply drag your finger up and down to scroll through a web page. If you need to zoom in on something, there are 2 different ways. To zoom in on a specific paragraph or section of a web page, double tap with your finger on that section, and Safari should zoom in and center the screen automatically. To zoom in on a very specific spot of a web page, touch down on the screen with two fingers, with your two fingers being very close together. Then spread your fingers apart while remaining on the screen. To zoom back out, touch two fingers down on the screen again, only this time have the fingers start far apart, and pull the fingers in towards each other. (Figures 10.3.1 & 10.3.2)

Double tap with ONE finger on the screen, and Safari will attempt to zoom to a perfect fit, centered on the section you double-tapped.

To zoom out: touch down on the screen with TWO fingers, with the fingers spaced far apart. Then drag the two fingers together while remaining on the screen. Release when the fingers come together, or when you are satisfied with the zoom.

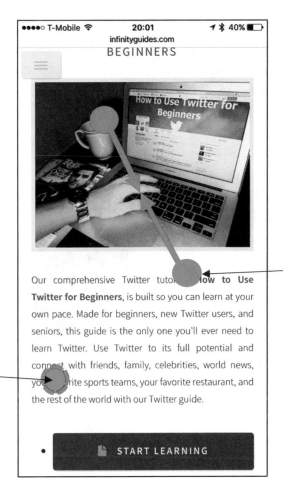

Figure 10.3.1 – Safari: Double Tap to Fit to Screen & Zoom Out

To zoom in: touch
down on the screen
with TWO fingers,
with the two fingers
being close together.
Then drag the fingers
away from each other
in opposite directions
while remaining on
the screen, releasing
at the end or when
you are satisfied with
the zoom.

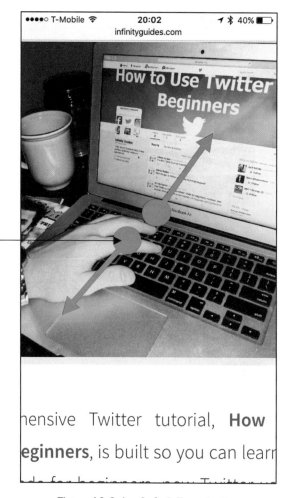

Figure 10.3.1 – Safari: Zooming In

You can still do all the basic functions of your normal web browser with Safari. To browse
through basic web functions, touch down at the bottom of your screen. This will bring up Safari
navigation options also known as web page controls (See Figure 10.1). From here, you can
browse as you please. For instance, to go back to the previous page, touch the left arrow. To go
forward a page, touch the right arrow. To manage a webpage, touch the rectangle with the
arrow in it. From here you have the options to mail the webpage to a friend, message the page
to a friend, tweet the page on your Twitter, share the page to Facebook, add a shortcut to the
web page to your home screen, print the web page, bookmark the page, or to add the page to
your reading list. (Figure 10.4) If you choose to bookmark the page, the page will appear in
your bookmarks screen which can be accessed by touching the book icon at the bottom of
Safari.

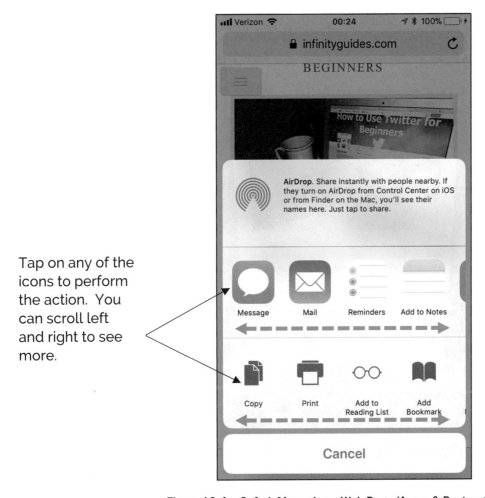

Tap on any of the icons to perform the action. You can scroll left and right to see more.

Figure 10.4 – Safari: Managing a Web Page (Arrow & Rectangle Icon)

Finally, you can browse in multiple tabs in Safari, by tapping the two windows icon at the bottom right of the Safari screen and then touching the plus icon. (Figure 10.5) Tabs are just additional browsing windows where you can browse the internet; an excellent tool for multi-taskers. To browse between tabs, touch the windows icon again. To truly master browsing through Safari, just take some time playing with it, and you will get it in no time.

Tap the x or swipe the page off the screen to close a tab.

Creates a new tab

Switches you to private browsing (does not save cookies or history)

Exits tab manager and returns to Safari main screen

Figure 10.5 – Safari: Using Tabs (Windows Icon-See Figure 10.1)

Chapter 11 – Using your Camera

Your iPhone is equipped with a powerful camera with flash capability. To access the camera, touch the <u>Camera app</u> on your home screen. There are a few options available inside the Camera app. On the top of your screen from left to right is: (<u>Figure 11.1</u>)

- **Lightning:** This turns flash to on, off, or auto.
- **HDR –** This enables or disables High Dynamic Range photography
- **Concentric Circles (if equipped) –** This enables or disables LIVE photos, which capture a second or so before and after the photo, thus creating what is called a "live photo."
- **Timer –** Tapping on this icon allows you to set a timer for the capture sequence.
- **Color Palette –** Allows you to choose a filter to capture the photo.

Taking a Photo

To take a photo, aim your camera and then tap on the <u>large circle icon</u> at the bottom of your screen. You can also turn your iPhone to the side to take a picture in landscape mode. Furthermore, you can use the selfie lens, which faces directly back at you, by tapping on the <u>camera icon</u> at the lower right of your screen. (<u>Figure 11.1</u>)

Camera Options

You can switch between different camera modes by tapping down somewhere on your <u>screen</u> while in the Camera app, and then swiping to the left and the right. You will notice different text become highlighted right above the capture icon to indicate which mode you are in. (<u>Figure 11.1</u>)

The different modes are:

- **Photo –** Standard photo mode
- **Video –** Records a video
- **Slo-Mo –** Records a video in slow motion
- **Time-Lapse –** Records a time lapse sequence
- **Square –** Captures a photo in a perfect square
- **Pano –** Captures a panoramic photo.

You can preview the photo you have just taken by tapping on the <u>preview of the photo</u> at the lower left of your screen. To get back to the camera from this preview, tap <u>Camera</u> at the upper left.

Camera Options

Tap on screen and swipe left or right to switch between camera modes

Camera Modes (highlighted is current mode)

Recent Photo Preview (tap to load)

Switch between regular and selfie lens

Capture Icon (tap to take picture or record video)

<u>Figure 11.1</u> – Camera App

Chapter 12 – Photos & Videos

Now that we know how to take photos and record videos, it is time to learn what we can do with these. All of your photos and videos can be found in the <u>Photos app</u>, which is located somewhere on your home screen.

Photos App Layout

See (<u>Figure 12.1</u>)

When you first open the Photos app, it may look like there is a lot going on. Let's take a look at navigating this expansive app. At the bottom will be your browsing tabs. The <u>Photos</u> tab will show you all of your photos. You can browse through these by scrolling up and down. <u>Memories</u> will show a specific memory, which are automatically generated by your device. An example of a memory is a photo you took one year ago from today. The <u>Shared</u> tab will bring you to shared photo streams, which we will discuss a little later on. Lastly, the <u>Albums</u> tab will bring you to all of your albums. At any time you can view a photo in full-screen by tapping on it.

Create a new
album

Manage albums
(deletion, etc.)

Browsing Tabs

Figure 12.1 – Photos App -> Albums Tab

iCloud Photo Library

Before we explore the Photos app more thoroughly, it's important to discuss what is called iCloud Photo Library. Photos take up a lot of hard drive space on your iPhone. Videos take up even more space. Your iPhone is equipped with what is called iCloud Photo Library, which basically stores your photos off of your iPhone and in the cloud, which is just a hard drive that is stored on the internet. iCloud Photo Library may be a great option for you if you plan on keeping a lot of photos on your iPhone. In order to use iCloud Photo Library your Apple ID must be set up, which we covered at the beginning of this book. If you want to enable iCloud Photo Library, follow these steps:

1. Open Settings app
2. Find Photos and tap it
3. At the top, tap on iCloud Photo Library to the right to enable it (green will show).
4. Choose whether you want to Optimize iPhone Storage or download the originals.

(Optimize storage will save you space)

5. You will now be using iCloud Photo Library.

It may take some time for your iPhone to upload all of your photos into the cloud.

Browsing Photos

Back inside the <u>Photos app</u>, let us browse around. The two best tabs at the bottom for browsing photos are Photos and Albums. If you tap on the <u>Photos</u> tab, all of your photos will be sorted by date. You can use the <u>back arrow</u> at the upper left to expand your view. (<u>Figure 12.2</u>)

Back arrow
(expand view)

Manage photos
(delete and
select multiple)

Figure 12.2 – Photos App -> Photos Tab

Tapping on the <u>Albums</u> tab, you can browse all of your photos as thumbnails by tapping on the <u>All Photos</u> album. To view a photo, tap on *it* to bring it full screen. Use the <u>back arrow</u> at the upper left to go back. (Figure 12.1)

To Create an Album

(See Figure 12.1)

1. Tap the Albums tab in Photos
2. Tap the plus sign at the upper left (If you do not see this, tap on Albums again)
3. Type in your new album name and tap Save
4. Scroll through your photos and tap each one you want to add to the album
5. Once you've selected all the photos you want, tap Done at the upper right

To Edit an Album

1. Open the album you want to edit in the Albums tab by tapping on *it*
2. Tap Select or Edit at the upper right
3. Tap each photo you want to manage within the album
4. Use the options at the bottom of your screen

Sharing a Photo

(See Figure 12.3)

To share a photo, follow these steps:

1. Find the photo you want to share, and tap on it to bring it full screen. (Note: You can select multiple photos by tapping Select at the upper right).
2. Tap the rectangle with the arrow in it at the lower left.
3. Tap on the corresponding option as to how you want to share it. (Message, Mail, Facebook, etc.)

Figure 12.3 – Sharing a Photo

Deleting Photos

1. Tap on the photo you want to delete (or select multiple by tapping on <u>Select</u> at the upper right).
2. Tap the <u>trash icon</u> at the lower right to delete.

Editing a Photo
(See <u>Figure 12.4</u>)

Remove red-
eye

Auto-adjust

Editing options

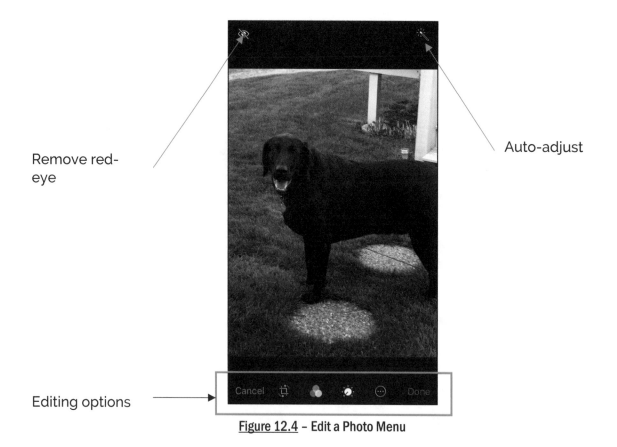

Figure 12.4 – Edit a Photo Menu

You can edit a photo in multiple ways, here's how:

1. Tap on the photo you want to edit to bring it full screen.
2. Tap <u>Edit</u> at the upper right. (For iOS 10: Tap the <u>3 lines and circles icon</u> at the bottom of your screen.)
   a. You can crop the photo by tapping on the <u>crop icon</u> at the bottom of your screen. Then use your fingers and drag the border to determine the crop. You can rotate the photo using the <u>block and arrow icon</u>. Tap the <u>crop icon</u> again to return. (<u>Figure 12.5</u>)

Tap and drag the corners of the picture until your desired crop has been reached. Tap Done when finished.

Rotate photo

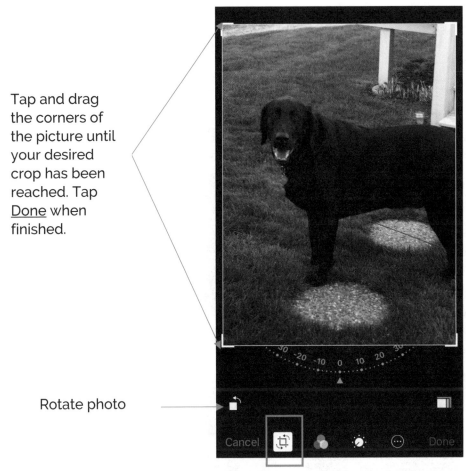

Figure 12.5 – Cropping and Rotating a Photo

b. You can add a filter to the photo by tapping on the <u>color palette icon</u>. (<u>Figure 12.6</u>)

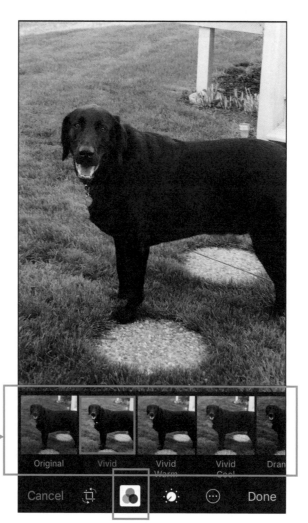

Tap on a filter
choice to add
the filter. Tap
Done when
finished.

Figure 12.6 – Adding a filter to a photo

c. You can alter lighting and shading of the photo by tapping on the sun icon.
    (Figure 12.7)

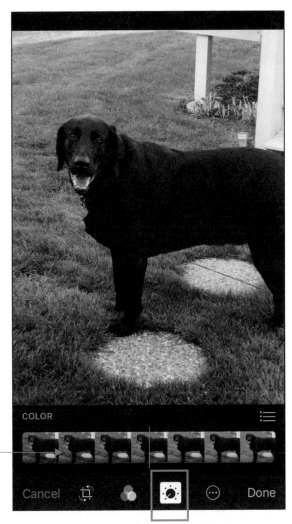

Drag the slider
to the desired
setting

Figure 12.7 – Adjusting Lighting and Color Settings of a Photo

    d. You can markup the photo by tapping on <u>the 3 dots within the circle icon</u>. Tap
        <u>Markup</u>. (<u>Figure 12.8</u>)

Using markup, you can write directly on the picture by placing your finger on the photo and drawing with your finger.

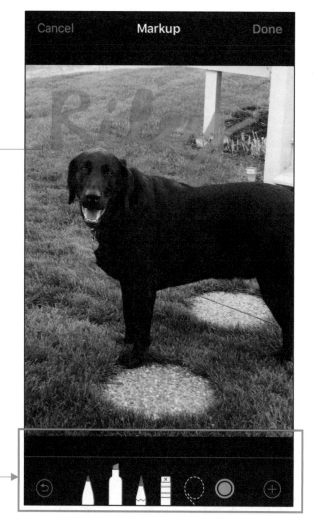

Markup Options

Figure 12.8 – Marking up a photo

    e. Tap Done when finished with Markup.

    f. You can remove red-eye by tapping on the <u>eye icon</u> at the upper left.

3. Tap <u>Done</u> on your screen when you are done editing the photo.

Photo Streams

A Photo Stream allows you to share a select set of photos with your friends who use Apple devices. To create a new Photo Stream:

1. Tap the <u>Shared tab</u> at the bottom inside the <u>Photos app</u>.

2. Tap the <u>back arrow</u> at the upper left.

3. Tap the <u>+</u> sign at the upper left.

4. Name your shared album.

5. Tap <u>Next</u> in the box.
6. Enter in the contacts you want to share the album with one at a time. NOTE: They must be Apple Device users.
7. Tap <u>Create</u> when done.
8. A notification will be sent to all of the contacts you entered.

When you receive an invitation to a shared Photo Stream, the Photos app will notify you and you can join the Photo Stream from the <u>Shared</u> tab.

Chapter 13 – iPhone Security

Security is a very important feature of the iPhone. As I emphasized early on in this book, it is extremely important to remember your lock screen passcode. If you forget this passcode, it is extremely tedious to get into your device. Doing so actually involves resetting your device to factory conditions, which will delete all your data. In this chapter I will show you how to change the security settings of your iPhone, including your lock screen passcode. Also, please remember your lock screen passcode is different from your Apple ID password.

Settings

All of your security settings can be viewed and changed inside the Settings app. We have used the Settings app several times already in this guide so you should have no problem by now finding and opening the Settings app. As a reminder, the Settings app can be found on your home screen, and you can open it by tapping on it with your finger.

Here inside the Settings app is where you can alter all the under the hood aspects of your iPhone. We will explore more in Settings later on, but for now, locate Touch ID & Passcode in Settings and tap on it. (Note: iPhones that do not have Touch ID capability will just show Passcode, you also may have to look inside General inside Settings to find it).

To get into Touch ID & Passcode you will have to enter your current Passcode. You may have set one up when you first setup your iPhone. Enter in your passcode and you will be brought to a new screen.

In this new screen you can alter many settings. You can choose whether to use Touch ID, change your passcode, or even turn your passcode off. Let's explore these. (Figure 13.1)

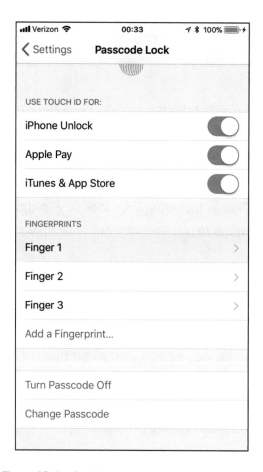

Figure 13.1 – Settings -> Touch ID & Passcode

Touch ID

Touch ID allows you to use your fingerprint to unlock your device. It also allows you to use your fingerprint for some other security measures, such as confirming a purchase of an app or song. To turn on and use Touch ID, if you haven't done so already when you first setup your iPhone, follow these steps. (If you already use Touch ID, you can use these steps to add an additional finger). From within Settings -> Touch ID & Passcode:

1. Tap <u>Add a Fingerprint</u>.
2. Now follow the instructions on the screen.
3. Once it's done, tap <u>Complete/Continue</u> at the bottom.
4. Your fingerprint will now be valid to unlock your device.

*Please note that when you use Touch ID, you will still be required to have a passcode set as well. This passcode will be required whenever your restart your iPhone or if Touch ID fails.

Passcode

Your passcode is a password that allows you to unlock your iPhone. Unlocking is simply the process of getting into your iPhone to use it. You should use a passcode for your iPhone. Otherwise, anyone will be able to get into your iPhone and have access to all of your data should they ever get possession of your iPhone.

Setting or Changing a Passcode

1. Within Touch ID & Passcode in Settings, tap Turn Passcode On or Change Passcode.
2. If you are changing your passcode, you will be required to enter your current passcode. Do so.
3. Now you can enter a new passcode. The standard is a 6-digit passcode, however many people prefer to use 4-digits or even an alphanumeric code. I personally prefer to use 4-digits. To change the type of passcode you want, tap on Passcode Options.
4. Now you can choose which type of passcode you want.
5. Tap in your new passcode.
6. Confirm the new passcode by tapping it in again.
7. Follow the instructions on the screen to finish entering your passcode.
8. When complete your passcode will be changed or set.

To Turn Off Passcode Completely

1. Within Touch ID & Passcode in Settings, tap Turn Passcode Off.
2. Tap Turn Off
3. Enter in your current passcode.

As a final reminder, you can use your passcode to unlock your iPhone from the sleep state. You can also use your fingerprint to unlock your iPhone from the sleep state if your iPhone has the capability.

Chapter 14 – Personal Settings

There are a number of personal settings you can set on your iPhone, and in this chapter we will explore some of them.

Setting your Wallpapers

Your wallpaper is just your background image on your iPhone. You have 2 different wallpapers: your home screen and your lock screen. To set your wallpapers follow these steps:

1. Open the Settings app.
2. Tap Wallpaper.
3. Tap Choose a New Wallpaper.
4. You can now choose between Dynamic, Stills, Live, and one of your Photos. Dynamic wallpapers are animated on your screen. Stills are not animated and are pre-loaded on the iPhone. Live wallpapers are animated when you press down on them using 3D Touch (More on 3D touch later). You can select one of your current photos by browsing through your albums at the bottom. (Figure 14.1)

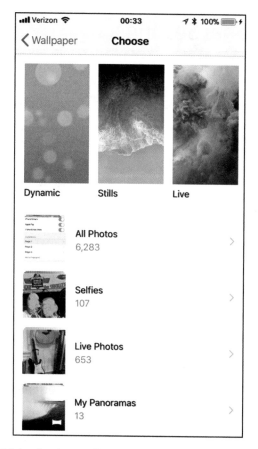

Figure 14.1 – Settings -> Wallpaper -> Choose a New Wallpaper

5. Select a photo to use as your wallpaper.
6. Select if you want the wallpaper to be Perspective or Still. Perspective adjusts to which angle you are viewing your iPhone at.
7. Tap Set.
8. Choose to set the wallpaper as your Lock Screen, Home Screen, or Both.

Ringtones & Vibrations

You can customize your ringtones and vibration settings in multiple ways. Here's how:

1. Open Settings.
2. Tap Sounds & Haptics.
3. Here you can adjust various sound settings such as ringer volume. To change a specific tone, such as your ringtone, tap on Ringtone.
4. Now you can tap on each tone to preview it on your iPhone. Once you have found the tone you want, use the back arrow at the upper left to go back.

5. You can adjust the vibration pattern of a tone by selecting the tone type (i.e. <u>Ringtone</u>) then tapping <u>Vibration</u> at the top.

6. Now you can tap each vibration pattern to preview it. Once you have found the pattern you like, use the <u>back arrow</u> at the upper left to go back.

Other Settings

You can adjust other personalized settings from within the Settings app. We will not cover them here in this text but feel free to check out <u>Display & Brightness</u> and <u>Battery</u> settings.

Chapter 15 – The Home Screen

By now, you should be pretty familiar with your home screen. As a reminder, your home screen is the main screen of your iPhone that shows all of your apps. You have multiple home screens, and you can switch between them by tapping down with your finger on the screen and swiping left or right. To get back to the main home screen at any time, simply press the home button. (See Figure 4.1 in Chapter 4 as a reminder)

3D Touch

3D Touch, also commonly referred to as Force Touch, is a feature on your iPhone that allows you to perform different functions while pressing down on your screen with different pressure. This is a fairly new feature of the iPhone and has not become widely used yet. Let's try it out and see what we can do. 3D Touch is not available on the iPhone 6 or older phones. If you have an iPhone 6 or earlier, you can skip the 3D Touch section.

3D Touch Example 1: On Apps

1. On your home screen, locate the Messages app.
2. Instead of tapping and releasing the Messages app to open it, tap down on it with some additional finger pressure and hold down for a moment.
3. You should feel your iPhone vibrate and a small popup window will appear (Figure 15.1)
4. Now, you can release your finger.
5. The screen that appears shows some recent contacts you have exchanged text messages with. You can tap on any of their names to immediately be brought to that particular messages thread.
6. You can return to your home screen by pressing the home button.

You can use 3D Touch on just about every app. Try it out on other apps to see which shortcuts appear.

By pressing down on the Messages app with a little extra force and holding for a moment, this screen will appear, allowing you to quickly go to a recent Messages thread

Figure 15.1 – 3D Touch on the Messages App

3D Touch Example 2: Photos

1. Open the Photos App.
2. Find a photo you want to quickly examine and instead of tapping on it normally, tap down and press with some pressure, and do not release your finger.
3. This will open a quick preview of the photo. If the photo is a Live Photo, it will play through it. Furthermore, if you selected a video, this will play the video.
4. If you release your finger, the preview will disappear. If while holding down, you slide your finger upwards and release, some options will appear. (Figure 15.2)
5. The shortcuts that appear are pretty useful, especially the copy function.

This is another example of how you can use 3D Touch. Try using it within other apps as well.

Tap to copy the photo, to be pasted later

Tap to add the photo to your favorites

Tap to share the photo

Tap to show other photos taken that day

Tap to delete photo

Figure 15.2 – 3D Touch an a Photo Thumbnail

Organizing Apps

Now that we learned how to use 3D Touch, let us move on to how we can organize our home screen. On your home screens, you can choose where you want each app to appear. You can also group multiple apps together in a folder.

Moving Apps Around on your Home Screen (Figure 15.3)

1. With light pressure, tap and hold down on an app on your home screen until all of your apps start to shake, then release your finger. (If a 3D Touch popup appears, you will have to try again, with lighter finger pressure).
2. Now that your apps are shaking, you are allowed to move the apps around.
3. To move an app, tap down on a shaking app and do not let go. You can now drag your finger anywhere on the screen to move the app to a new location.
4. To move the app to a new home screen, drag the app all the way to the right or left and hold it there, until the home screen changes. Press the home button to return.

Grouping Apps into Folders (Figure 15.3)

1. With light pressure, tap and hold down on an app on your home screen until all of your apps start to shake, then release your finger.
2. If you want to create a folder of apps on your home screen, tap down on an app and hold it, then drag it on top of another app that you want to group with the app you are holding.
3. You will see a small window appear behind your app. Release your finger.
4. A new folder has just been created. Your iPhone will name the folder for you. To change the name of the folder, tap into the box and use your keyboard to enter in a name.
5. Tap out of the folder to return to the home screen with your apps still shaking.
6. You can organize that folder the same way you can organize apps. You can move more apps into that folder by tapping, holding, and dragging apps into the folder. Press the home button to return.

How to Delete Apps (Figure 15.3)

1. With light pressure, tap and hold down on an app on your home screen until all of your apps start to shake, then release your finger.
2. To delete an app, tap the small (x) that appears at the upper left of an app.
3. Then tap Delete.
4. To delete a folder, just move all the apps inside a folder out of that folder.
5. Please note that some apps that came with the iPhone cannot be deleted.
6. Once an app is deleted, you can always get it back in the App Store, which is covered in the next chapter.

Tap the small "x" to delete the app

Drag and drop with your finger one app to inside another app to create a folder on your home screen.

Drag and drop an app with your finger to another location on your home screen to move it there

Drag an app with your finger to the edge of your screen to move it to another home screen

Figure 15.3 – Managing & Organizing Apps

Chapter 16 – Apps

Everything that your iPhone can do are functions of apps. When you make a phone call, you are using the Phone app. When you send a text message, you are using the Messages app. When you browse the Internet, you are using the Safari app. Even when you are changing your settings, you are using the Settings app. The apps that come with the iPhone are extraordinarily useful, but these are just a blade of grass in a field compared to the vast amount of apps available. To get new apps, you will need to use an app called the App Store, which is located somewhere on your home screen.

App Store

Let's open the App Store by tapping on it on our home screen. In order to use the App Store, you must have an Apple ID and you must be signed in to your Apple ID on your iPhone. If you still have not set up your Apple ID yet, I urge you to do so. See Chapter 5 on setting up your Apple ID.

Browsing the App Store

(See Figure 16.1)

Here in the App Store you can browse through the massive library of apps available for download. Again, make sure you are signed in with your Apple ID, and make sure you remember your Apple ID password as you will need it to download apps.

Here at the main page of the App Store, called the Today page, you can see all the new and featured apps that Apple recommends. Let's take a look at the layout of this page, and the App Store itself, particularly the tabs at the bottom.

- **Today** – The Today tab shows you exactly what you see now, featured apps and content.
- **Games** – This tab allows you to browse game apps.
- **Apps** – This tab allows you to browse through all apps available.
- **Updates** – Shows you if any updates are available for apps.
- **Search** – Allows you to search for a specific app or function of an app.

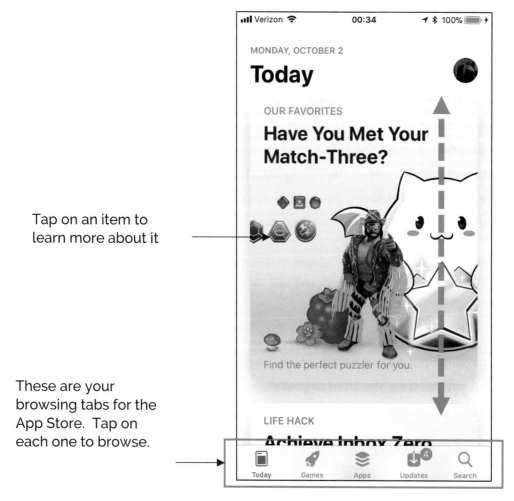

Tap on an item to learn more about it

These are your browsing tabs for the App Store. Tap on each one to browse.

Figure 16.1 – The App Store -> Today Tab

Browsing By Category

One of the best ways to find good apps is to browse by category. To do this, first tap the Apps tab at the bottom, then scroll down until you see Top Categories (Figure 16.2). Some categories will be shown and you can tap on one to explore it. For now, tap on See All to view all app categories.

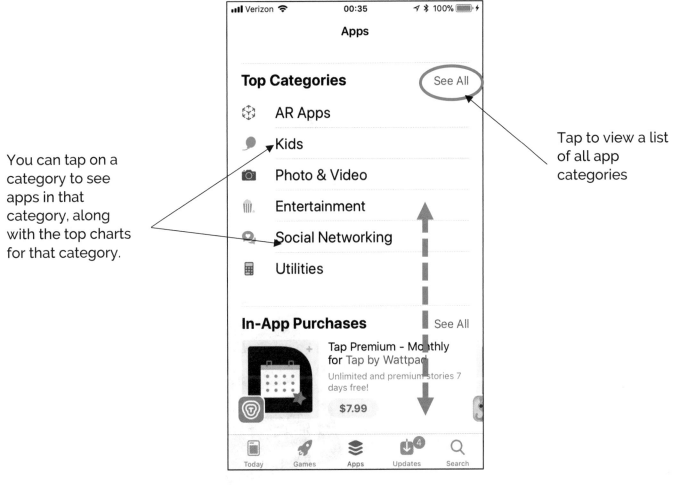

You can tap on a category to see apps in that category, along with the top charts for that category.

Tap to view a list of all app categories

Figure 16.2 – The App Store -> Apps Tab -> Top Categories

When viewing all categories, you can scroll up and down to see the full list. Simply tap on a category to see apps within it. Within each category page, you will see Apps that are recommended by curators and the top charts for that category. The top charts include the most downloaded and used apps in that category and they are sort by free apps and paid apps. Paid apps are apps you have to pay for in order to download. As always, you can use the back arrows at the upper left to go back.

Viewing an App

(See Figure 16.3)

When you see an app that interests you, you can tap on the app itself to view more information. On this screen you will see the name of the app, the price to download it if there is one, and you will see the app's user ratings, rankings, age recommendation, and more. By scrolling down and scrolling left and right you can see screenshots of the app, read a description of the app, and read user ratings and reviews.

User ratings (average star rating), app rank, and age recommendation

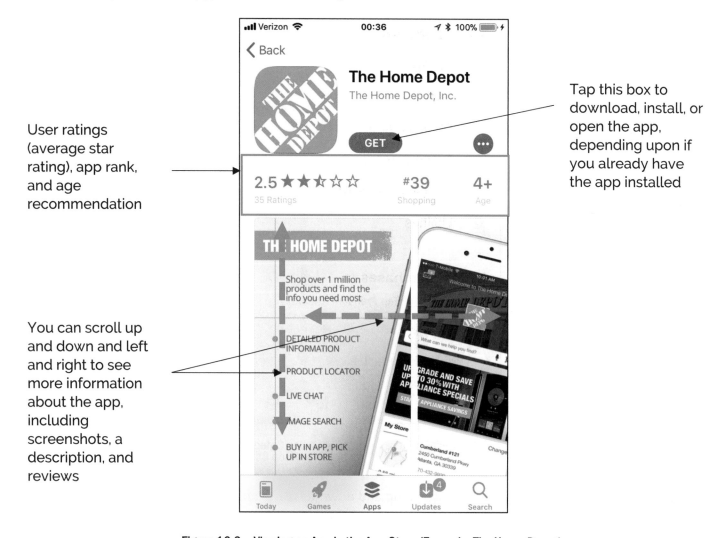

Tap this box to download, install, or open the app, depending upon if you already have the app installed

You can scroll up and down and left and right to see more information about the app, including screenshots, a description, and reviews

Figure 16.3 – Viewing an App in the App Store (Example: The Home Depot)

Top Charts

(See Figure 16.4)

Using Top Charts is one of my favorite ways to find popular apps. We have already demonstrated how to view Top Charts for categories, but you can also see Top Charts for all apps regardless of category. To access these Top Charts, first make sure you are on the Apps tab. Then, scroll down until you come upon the headlines **Top Paid** and **Top Free**. These two sections show you the most downloaded and used paid and free apps. You can tap on See All to see the full list, and you can tap on any app to learn more information.

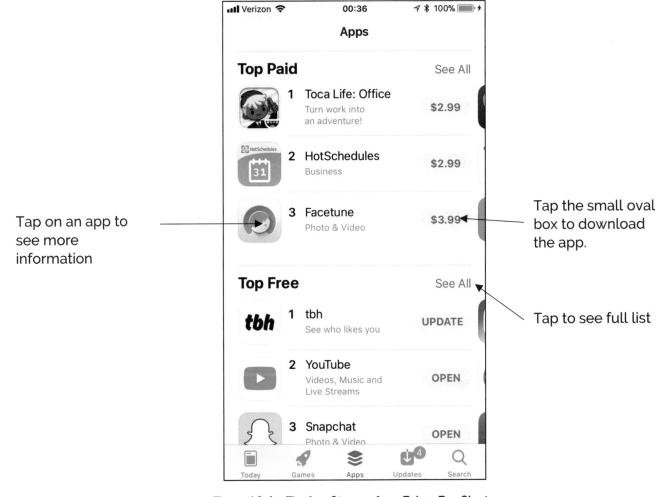

Tap on an app to see more information

Tap the small oval box to download the app.

Tap to see full list

Figure 16.4 – The App Store -> Apps Tab -> Top Charts

Searching for Apps

If you know the specific app you want to download, you can search for it using the Search tab at the bottom. Tapping on this tab will allow you to search for any app by tapping into the search bar at the top of the screen. Simply type in the name of the app, or a subject such as "photo" and tap search on your keyboard. Usually, when you type the search term into the search field the App Store will make suggestions as to what you are looking for. You can tap on that suggestion to quickly enter it in and search. Now you will see a list returning your search results, and you can view these apps by tapping on them.

Updates

(See Figure 16.5)

The Updates tab shows you what updates, if any, are available for apps you already own. You can tap Update next to the app to install the update. Alternatively, you can tap Update All at the upper right to install all available updates.

The updates tab will also show updates recently installed. You can also set your apps to update automatically. We will cover this later on.

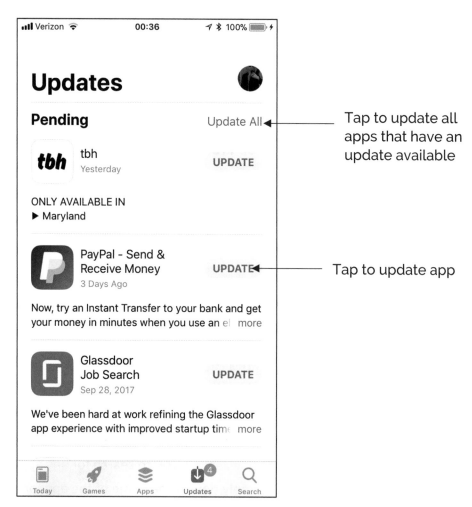

Figure 16.5 – The App Store -> Updates Tab

Downloading Apps

Now that we have seen how we can browse apps, let us see how we actually download one to our iPhone. The process is actually pretty simple, but before we begin let me give a note on your Apple ID.

As emphasized earlier in this chapter, in order to use the App Store you must be signed in with your Apple ID. You are also going to need your Apple ID password to download apps. On occasion, your iPhone will ask for this password just for verification purposes. Lastly, you will need credit card information linked to your Apple ID in order to download certain apps. Adding your credit card information is fairly simple. Your iPhone will ask you when it needs this information, and will bring up a screen with directions. Adding your credit card data does not mean you will be charged. Apple just needs it IN CASE you decide to purchase something.

Here is how you download an app:

1. Open the App Store.
2. Find the app you want to download.
3. Next to the app will be a box. Inside this box will be the words GET or a price such as $0.99. If the box says OPEN, then you already have the app downloaded. (See Figure 16.4)
4. Tap this box.
5. *iOS 10 Only*: Next tap the same box again. This time the words INSTALL may be in the box.
6. You may be asked for your Apple ID password at this point or Touch ID. Enter it in.
7. You may be asked to update your billing information at this point, such as credit card and billing address. Enter it in if prompted.
8. Your download will now commence. When it is finished, your newly downloaded app will appear on your home screen somewhere.

Using Downloaded Apps

When you download an app, it will appear on your home screen. To open it, just tap it. Using an app from the App Store is the same as any using any app that comes with the iPhone. You can usually scroll through screens on the app, tap icons, and more. Each app is unique to itself, so you will have to play around with the app to get the hang of it.

There are certain aspects of apps that are important to consider. The first is in-app purchases. Many apps allow you to buy features or items from directly inside the app. These purchases could be access to content or even physical goods. To make these purchases you will be using your Apple ID. Another aspect is advertisements. Some apps have advertisements running through them. For most apps these are non-conspicuous and do not interfere with using the app, but for others the advertisements can be quite bothersome. If an app is flooded with advertisements and popups that make it difficult to even use the app, I would consider deleting the app and using something else. Apps like these are just trying to spam you with advertisements rather than provide a good service.

It is also worth noting that some apps offer a paid and free version. Usually the paid version comes with extra features or no advertisements.

Resources for Learning How to use Apps

You can check out the appendix of this text for a list of popular and useful apps. You'd be amazed at what types of apps are out there and what they can do.

Some apps are a little tricky to learn, and there are a plethora of resources out there to help you. For learning how to use certain apps, we recommend checking out www.infinityguides.com. That website is dedicated to teaching people how to use many popular apps from a beginner's perspective.

Chapter 17 – Notifications

So far we have covered all the basics of using the iPhone. You now know how to navigate the iPhone, make phone calls, exchange text messages, browse the Internet, use your email, personalize your device, download apps, and more. Now we are going to get into specific features that are absolutely essential to understand, and we start with Notifications.

Overview

Notifications are an integral part of your iPhone. Every time you receive a text, you will receive a notification. Every time you miss a phone call, you will receive a notification. In fact, every time certain information is delivered to you from an app, you will receive what is called a notification.

Notifications appear on your iPhone in several forms. On your lock screen, you will see notifications lined up (Figure 17.1). While using your iPhone, you will see notifications in real-time pop up at the top of your screen (Figure 17.2). When these notifications appear, you can tap on it to be brought directly to the notification. For instance, if you receive a text message while you are doing something on your iPhone, a box will appear at the top of your screen showing the text message and who it is from. This box will appear briefly. While the box is there, you can tap on it to be brought directly into the thread of the text message so you can respond. Alternatively, you can tap that box and drag your finger down to reply immediately.

Another type of notification is the badge icon, which is simply the red bubble you can see above an app on the home screen that has a number in it. This usually means you have a certain number of notifications available for that particular app. For instance, your Messages app will show a number in a red bubble above it on your home screen. This number indicates how many unread text messages you currently have.

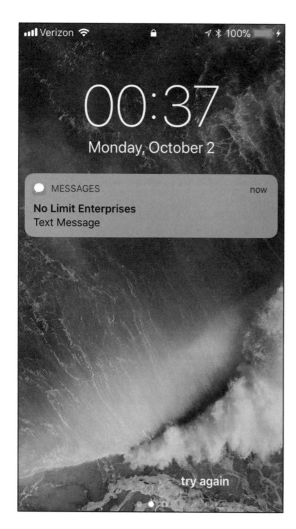

Figure 17.1 – Notifications on the Lock Screen

Figure 17.2 – Notifications while iPhone Unlocked

Notifications can also appear in real-time as an alert. An alert is larger box that appears in the middle of your screen and they usually require you to dismiss the notification before it goes away. An example of this is the alarm clock notification on your iPhone.

The Notification Panel

At any time you can view all of your current notifications by accessing the Notification Panel. To do this, tap down at the very top of your screen at any time and swipe your finger down. This is your Notification Panel (Figure 17.3).   Here you can see all the notifications that you have not acknowledged. To go to a particular notification, simply tap on it. To clear out a section of notifications, tap the small x next to the date, and then tap clear. Just press the home button to return to your home screen.

To open the
Notification Panel,
tap down at the
very top of your
screen and swipe
down

Tap and swipe to
the right to
quickly open the
notification (or
just tap on the
notification)

Tap to clear the
particular set of
notifications

Tap and swipe to
the left to view the
complete
notification or clear
it. Swiping
completely to the
left will clear the
notification.

Figure 17.3 – The Notification Panel (Center)

Examples of Notifications

As stated earlier, a notification can be from any app. For instance, a breaking news story from
Fox News can be a notification if you have the Fox News app. A new Facebook like on your post
can be a notification if you have the Facebook app installed. Basically, any app can deliver
notifications.

Managing Notifications

Sometimes, you may not want to get notifications from a certain app. These can be easily
managed in the Settings app.

1. Open the Settings app.
2. Tap Notifications.
3. Tap the app you want to manage notifications for.
4. Now you can choose whether you want to allow notifications from this app. You can also choose the type of notification as well as some other options. (Figure 17.4)

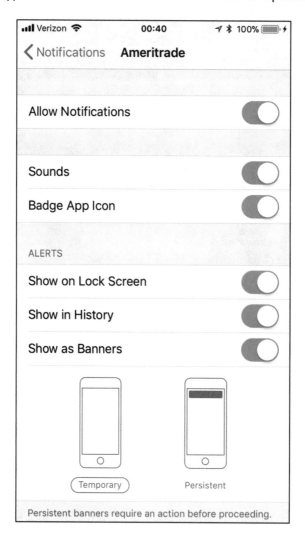

Figure 17.4 – Settings -> Notifications -> App Name (Ameritrade)

Chapter 18 – The Control Center

The Control Center, sometimes referred to as the "control panel," is a nifty tool on the iPhone that allows you to quickly change some settings. Let's explore it.

To Access the Control Center

1. On any screen on your iPhone, tap down at the very bottom of your screen and swipe up. You will now see the Control Center (Figure 18.1). [For iOS 10, see Figure 18.2]

Turn cellular data on/off

Airplane mode

Turn Wi-Fi on/off

Turn Bluetooth on/off

Lock/Unlock orientation

Turn Do Not Disturb on/off

Quick music controls

Adjust brightness

Adjust volume

To open the Control Center, tap down at the very bottom of your screen and swipe up

Figure 18.1 – The Control Center

Turn Bluetooth on/off

Turn Wi-Fi on/off

Airplane mode

Turn Do Not Disturb on/off

Lock/Unlock orientation

Adjust brightness

To open the Control Center, tap down at the very bottom of your screen and swipe up

Figure 18.2 – The Control Center (iOS 10 Only)

Control Center Functions

Inside your Control Center you will see some buttons. Tapping these buttons turns the selected setting on or off.

- **Airplane Mode –** Tapping on the airplane button turns airplane mode on or off. When a button is highlighted that means it is currently enabled. Airplane mode turns off all communication abilities on the iPhone, including cellular, Wi-Fi, and Bluetooth. Once you turn Airplane mode on, you can still enable Wi-Fi by using the Control Center.
- **Wi-Fi –** The radio waves is the Wi-Fi button. Tapping this will turn Wi-Fi on or off.

- **Cellular Data** – The antenna icon enabled or disables cellular data. (iOS 11 Only)
- **Bluetooth** – The Bluetooth button turns Bluetooth on or off. To connect to a Bluetooth device, you need to go to Settings -> Bluetooth.
- **Do Not Disturb** – The moon button enables or disables Do Not Disturb mode. When you enable Do Not Disturb mode, you will not receive notifications or hear any sounds for phone calls and messages. These along with all other notifications besides your alarm clock will be silenced.
- **Lock Orientation** – The lock orientation button will lock the orientation of your iPhone in portrait mode. When this is enabled, turning your iPhone to landscape orientation will not re-orientate the screen. If your iPhone screen is not orientating to landscape mode this option may be on.
- **Screen Mirroring** – This button lets you mirror your iPhone's screen to an Apple TV. (For iOS 10 this is AirPlay Mirroring)

On the right side of the Control Center are two vertical ovals for brightness and volume. You can adjust these settings by tapping in the oval and dragging up or down to increase or decrease the brightness or volume. (For iOS 10, the brightness slider is horizontal and the Volume slider can be accessed by swiping to the left)

Music Controls

The Music box in the Control Center allows you to quickly control your music. While a track is playing, you can bring up the Control Center and then use the skip back, pause/play, and skip forward icons to quickly navigate through your music without having to open up the Music app. You can also bring up more options such as broadcasting to a Bluetooth connected speaker by tapping on the sound wave icon at the upper right of the Music box. Simply tap out of the enlarged Music box or press the home button to return to the main Control Center. (For iOS 10, swipe to the left on the main Control Center to access music controls)

Control Center Apps

The bottom buttons in the Control Center open certain apps or perform functions.

- **Flashlight** – Tapping on the flashlight icon turns on your iPhone's flashlight, which is just the flash on your camera. Tap the flashlight again to turn it off. This function is very useful.
- **Timer/Alarm Clock** – The clock icon opens the Clock app, and brings you directly to the Timer. In the Timer, you can set a timer that will notify you when the desired time elapses with an alert and sound. You can also set your alarm clock from here by tapping

on the <u>Alarm</u> tab at the bottom. To create a new alarm, tap the <u>plus icon</u> at the upper right. Alternatively, you can enable a previously created alarm by tapping the <u>small oval</u> next to a time. You can now set the time for your alarm and specify which type of alert you want. Tap <u>Save</u> at the upper right to finish setting the alarm.

- **Calculator –** The third icon at the bottom is the Calculator app. Tap this to open up the calculator, which you can use.
- **Camera –** The last icon at the bottom opens the Camera app.

3D Touch Functions in the Control Center

You can use 3D Touch on almost all of the Control Center buttons. As a reminder, 3D Touch is pressing down on the screen with a little additional force and holding it for a moment. Two 3D Touch examples are worth noting in the Control Center:

- **Night Shift –** To enable Night Shift, press on the vertical brightness adjustor with a little additional force and hold until the adjustor comes to full screen. Underneath the adjustor will be the <u>Night Shift</u> button, which you can tap on to enable. When you turn Night Shift on, your iPhone will change its color display. The purpose of Night Shift is for when you are using your iPhone late at night and do not want your iPhone's screen straining your eyes and potentially keeping you awake. Night Shift will automatically turn off the next morning. (For iOS 10, Night Shift will have its own button in the main Control Center).
- **Flashlight –** Performing 3D Touch on the flashlight button allows you to adjust the power of the flashlight. Simply tap or drag your finger on the scale to adjust the power.

Exiting the Control Center

To exit the Control Center either press the <u>home button</u> or tap down on the Control Center and swipe it back down.

Chapter 19 – Siri

Siri, as you may have heard, is Apple's intelligent voice assistant. You can talk to Siri, and Siri will listen to what you say and try to do whatever you ask. The possibilities of what you can do with Siri are endless.

Turning Siri On

(See Figure 19.1)

By default, Siri is enabled on your iPhone. To be sure, let's make sure Siri is enabled. To do this, follow these steps:

1. Open Settings
2. Find and tap Siri & Search (Or just Siri for iOS 10)
3. Make sure Press Home for Siri is enabled at the top. (The slider tab next to it should be green. If not, tap it).

While we are in the Siri settings screen, let's take a quick look at some of the settings you can adjust.

- **Allow Siri When Locked** – Allows you to access Siri when your iPhone is locked. I usually leave this enabled so I can access Siri quickly without unlocking my iPhone.
- **Listen for "Hey Siri"** – With this enabled, you can access Siri by simply saying "Hey Siri" at any time. Personally, I don't use this option as there is a much more reliable way to access Siri.
- **Other Settings** – The settings at the bottom allow you to change some other settings including which language you want Siri to use and which voice you want Siri to have.

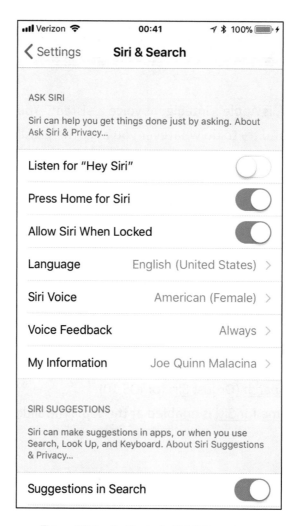

Figure 19.1 – Settings -> Siri & Search

Accessing Siri

Now that Siri is enabled on your iPhone, let's go back to the home screen. From the home screen accessing Siri is very easy. The easiest way to access Siri is to press and hold the home button until you see a sound wave appear at the bottom of your screen. (Figure 19.2)

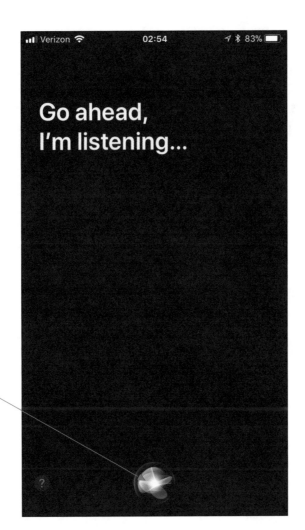

You can make Siri start listening again by pressing on the sound wave (or this icon shown), or pressing and holding the home button again

Figure 19.2 – Using Siri

Using Siri

Now let's try some examples to see exactly how Siri works. First, let me note that when you access Siri by holding the home button, you have two different approaches. One is, when the sound wave appears, you can let go of the home button and start speaking. Two is, when the sound wave appears, you can continue holding down on the home button, start speaking, and release the home button when you are done speaking. Either way works. For simplicity, I am going to use the former method in our examples.

So let's press and hold the <u>home button</u> until the sound wave appears then release the <u>home button</u>. Now we can say, "What is the weather?" Siri will listen, then respond with some information. She can either speak the information back to you or bring up a screen with the information you requested. To start a new Siri session or attempt to speak again, tap on the <u>graphic</u> that appears at the bottom of your screen. Or just hold the <u>home button</u> again.

Let's try another example, press and hold the <u>home button</u> and release, and then say "Show me my Photos." Siri will listen and then automatically open the Photos app for you.

There are countless things you can say to Siri that she will perform. Try out anything you'd like. A few more examples are listed below, and you can see a much larger list of examples in the appendix of this text.

- Make Phone Calls – "Call *Contact Name*"
- Lookup Contact Information – "Lookup *Contact Name*"
- Lookup Sports Scores – "Who won the White Sox game today?"
- Set an Alarm Clock – "Set an alarm for 6:30 AM"
- Do Math – "What is two plus two?"
- Visit Websites – "Bring me to Infinity Guides dot com"

Chapter 20 – Native Apps

Let's explore some native apps that come preloaded on the iPhone. Many of these are very useful and you may find yourself using them often.

Music

The Music app is where you can play and listen to your music. There are two ways to listen to music. The first is to load songs that you already own onto your iPhone. To do this, you will need to use iTunes, which is a program for computers. To see how to do this, go to www.infinityguides.com and search "iTunes".

The second way to listen to music is to use the Apple Music service. This service lets you listen to nearly any song you want at any time, right from your iPhone and any computer or device. The Apple Music service is huge, and is a subscription service from Apple. To learn how to use Apple Music, go to www.infinityguides.com and search "Apple Music".

Once you have music on your iPhone using any of the two above methods, using the Music app is pretty simple. You can browse through the app using the tabs at the bottom, and simply tap on a song to play it. You can also quickly skip through tracks in the Control Center, which is covered in Chapter 18.

Maps

The maps app is a great app for turn-by-turn navigation. In other words, it is a GPS right on your iPhone. Inside the Maps app you can tap into the search bar and type in the address of where you want to go. You can also search for nearby places. While typing an address or place, Maps will present suggestions as to what you are looking for. If yours comes up, you can tap on it. Tap on <u>Directions</u> to get driving directions to the location. Your iPhone will give you turn-by-turn directions as you are driving. (<u>Figure 20.1</u>)

Tapping this icon will show your current location

Enter address or place in here for directions

Figure 20.1 – Maps App

Note: There are other apps that offer GPS and turn-by-turn directions. Two popular ones are Google Maps and Waze, available in the App Store for free.

Weather

The Weather app is a very simple app that shows you the current weather and forecast. By default, the Weather app will show you your current location's weather, as long as you have Location Services enabled in Settings.

To add an area to the Weather app, tap the 3 lines at the bottom right. Now tap on the plus sign and you can enter a postal code to quickly add that area to your Weather app. You can browse through your different saved locations by swiping left or right. You can also scroll up and down to see additional weather information. (Figure 20.2)

Tap here to add
another location to
check weather

Figure 20.2 – Weather App

FaceTime

(See Figure 20.3)

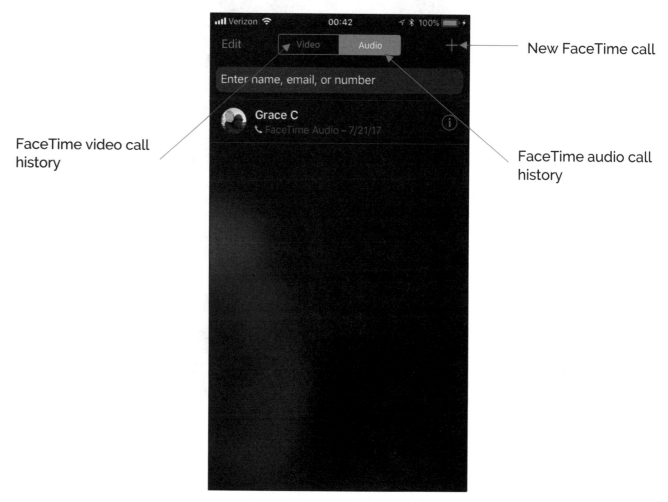

New FaceTime call

FaceTime video call
history

FaceTime audio call
history

Figure 20.3 – FaceTime App

FaceTime, which we have mentioned briefly earlier in this text, is an app that allows you to
partake in video calls with other Apple users. This app is very similar to Skype, which is also
available for free in the App Store. When you open FaceTime, you can place a video call by
tapping on the plus sign at the upper right. Now you can look through your contacts to find
someone to video chat with. When you have found that person, tap on their _name_. Now
FaceTime will determine if they are able to make a FaceTime call. You will know if you are able
to FaceTime that person because some icons may appear next to their name. If the video
recorder icon appears, that means that you can make a FaceTime video call with them. If the
phone icon appears next to their name that means you can make a FaceTime audio call with
them, which has no video. If both icons are greyed out, and you are not allowed to tap on

them, that means you cannot make a FaceTime call of any type with them. In other words, they do not have FaceTime on their device. (Figure 20.4)

FaceTime calls have pretty much the same controls as regular phone calls. You can adjust which camera you are using by tapping on the camera icon.

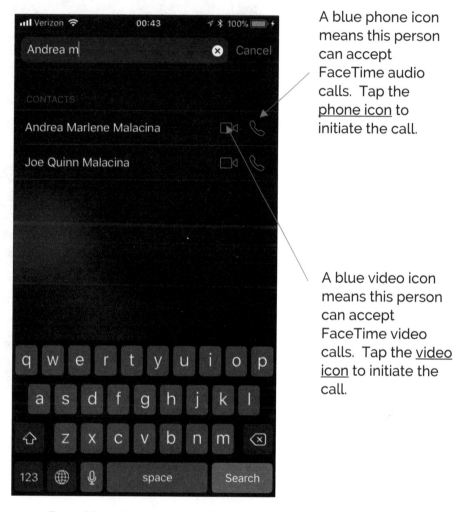

A blue phone icon means this person can accept FaceTime audio calls. Tap the phone icon to initiate the call.

A blue video icon means this person can accept FaceTime video calls. Tap the video icon to initiate the call.

Figure 20.4 – FaceTime Availability

 Clock

We have already covered most of the Clock app in Chapter 18. There are a few things we missed however, so we will cover them now. In this app you can see the time around the world, as well as set an alarm, and start a timer. You can also use the stopwatch function by tapping on the Stopwatch tab at the bottom. Lastly, the Bedtime tab allows you to set up a custom bedtime and wake-up alarm, depending upon how you sleep. (<u>Figure 20.5</u>)

Clock tabs for different functions (alarm clock, bedtime function, stopwatch, timer, and world clock)

<u>Figure 20.5</u> – Clock App

Notes

The Notes app is an incredibly useful app for creating notes. It is very easy to use; just open the <u>Notes</u> app, tap the <u>pencil and square icon</u> at the lower right to start a new note, and begin typing away. Notes save automatically, and you can access all of your saved notes in the main notes screen (use the <u>back arrows</u> at the upper left).   You can delete notes by tapping on <u>Edit</u> at the upper right.

Furthermore, while creating a note you can sketch and use additional tools by using the icons at the bottom of your screen. You can also password protect certain notes by opening the note, and tapping the <u>square and rectangle</u> at the upper right, and then tapping <u>lock note</u>. Notes save automatically. (<u>Figure 20.6</u>)

Tap on a note to open/view/edit it

Use to select multiple for management or deletion

Create new note

Figure 20.6 – Notes App

iBooks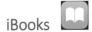

iBooks is the app that lets you read books on your iPhone. The iPhone screen is a little small, so this app may be better used on an iPad. All eBooks that you download and store in iCloud, or place in your device through iTunes will be available in iBooks.

You can also browse through books and download them using the tabs at the bottom of iBooks, including the Search and Top Charts tab. You will need to be signed in with your Apple ID to purchase and download books. Once you purchase a book using your Apple ID, it will automatically be sent to all of your Apple devices that are signed in with your Apple ID. So if you buy a book on your iPhone, it will also appear on your iPad for easy reading. You may even be reading this book on your iPad!

Calendar

(See Figure 20.7)

The Calendar app is a pretty simple app that allows you to create events and reminders. To view all the events you have on a day, simply tap on that day.

To Create a New Event

1.   Tap the plus icon at the upper right.
2.   Enter in all the corresponding information, if required. Include the date and time (if applicable).
3.   Choose whether you want to set an alarm to remind you about this event.
4.   When you are done, tap Add at the upper right.
5.   Your event has now been added to your calendar.

You can tell if you have scheduled events on a day if a dot appears below the date. You can tap on Today at the lower right to be brought to your Today view, which shows you which events you have coming up, starting with today.

You can also see a quick view of what you have coming up on your calendar from the home screen. Simply go to your home screen, and swipe your finger to the right until you get to the Today screen. If you have any events in your calendar coming up, they will appear here.

The dot means you have something scheduled on this date

Create new calendar event such as event, appointment, or meeting

Tap on a date to view it

View your upcoming events, as of today

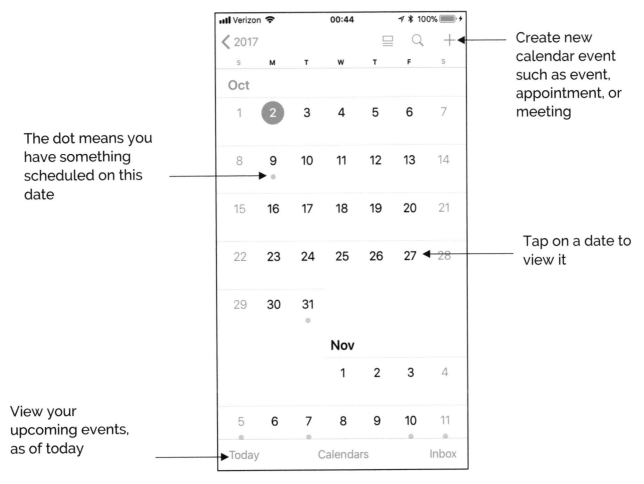

Figure 20.7 – Calendar App

Chapter 21 – Tips & Tricks

Congratulations! You have made it through the majority of this book, and you should now have a solid understanding of how to use your iPhone. There are no more "basics" left to teach you, so I will leave you with a few tips and tricks that you may find helpful when using your iPhone.

Backing up your Device

This is a MAJOR tip. You should always have a backup of your iPhone's data available in case anything happens. If you destroy or lose your iPhone, a backup will allow you to get all of your data back. There are two ways to back up your device.

1. Backup to iCloud (Recommended)

Backing up to iCloud is definitely the way to go. This is done automatically and continuously so you never have to worry about anything. You will need an Apple ID to do so, and you must be signed in to iCloud with that Apple ID (covered in first few chapters of book). To turn iCloud backup on, follow these steps:

1. Open Settings.
2. Tap the big box at the top with your name.
3. Tap iCloud.
4. Tap iCloud Backup.
5. Now make sure iCloud Backup is on (enabled green). If it was off previously, tap on Back Up Now to begin the backup.

When your iPhone is backing up to iCloud, you do not need to worry about setting up backup again, as your iPhone will backup periodically, usually when you are sleeping and your iPhone is charging. Please note your iPhone must be connected to Wi-Fi in order to initiate its automatic backup. Now should anything ever happen to your iPhone, you can always get your data back. iCloud saves your data securely in the cloud.

2. Backup to iTunes

The second way to backup your device is to use iTunes. Doing this saves a backup on your computer that can quickly be restored. To learn how to do this, visit www.infinityguides.com

and click on "Online Courses" and then "How to Use iTunes for Beginners".

Automatically Update Apps

I mentioned earlier in this text that I would show you how to set your iPhone to automatically update apps as updates came in. When this feature is on, you will not need to ever manually update apps through the App Store. Here are the steps:

1. Open Settings
2. Tap iTunes & App Store
3. Tap the button icon next to Updates under Automatic Downloads to enable it

Taking a Screenshot

A screenshot is a picture of exactly what your screen looks like, and can be very useful. For instance, say you received a text with instructions on how to bake a cake, and you want to share those instructions with a friend via text message. One way to accomplish this is take a screenshot of the original text and send the picture of that screenshot to your friend.

At any time you can take a screenshot of what you are viewing on your iPhone by pressing and holding the power button and home button for one second, at the same time. You will know a screenshot was taken when you see your screen flash, and the screenshot appears in the lower left corner of your screen. You can tap on the picture to view it, and several sharing and editing features will become available to you. Screenshots will save as pictures in your Photos app.

Background Apps
(See Figure 21.1)

Whenever you open an app, it remains open in the background even after you leave the app. It can be beneficial to close down all background apps to improve the speed and performance of your iPhone. You can also use this method to quickly go to an app you were recently using.

Tap down on an app screen, and swipe it up and off your screen to completely close it down.

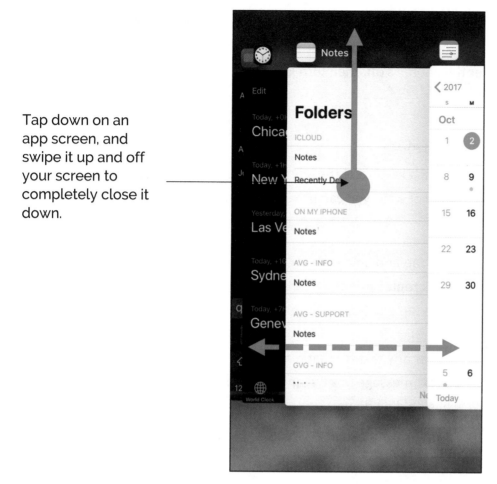

Figure 21.1 – Closing Background Apps (Double-press the home button quickly)

How to Close Background Apps OR Go to a Recent App

1. Double press the <u>home button</u> quickly. Your home screen should break away and you should see numerous screens next to each other.
2. If you want to quickly go to another app you used recently, swipe left or right and tap on the <u>screen of the app</u> you want to go to.
3. To close down an app, tap down on the <u>screen of the app</u>, and swipe it up and off the screen. This closes down an app completely.
4. Do this for each running app to close down all the background apps.
5. Press the <u>home button</u> to return when done.

Restart your iPhone

It is best practice to restart your iPhone every now and then, the same way you would restart a computer to keep it fresh. I recommend restarting your iPhone if it is running slow or not working properly. Doing so can fix the problem. As a good practice, I recommend restarting your iPhone at least twice a month. To do so, simply turn the iPhone off using the power button. Wait 60 seconds after the phone is off, then turn it back on.

3D Touch on Everything (If Applicable)

In Chapter 15, we covered the 3D touch feature of the iPhone (if you have an iPhone 6s or newer). Now I will show you a couple of ways you can use 3D Touch that may have slipped your thought process.

1. In the Messages app, you can tap and hold with some pressure to bring up a quick preview of a thread, and quick reply options. (Figure 21.2)
2. In the Control Center, you can tap and hold with some pressure on the Timer icon to quickly set a timer. (Figure 21.3)
3. When typing a text message, or any text for that matter, you can quickly move your text marker to anywhere in the text message box by tapping and holding with some pressure on the keyboard. Now, while holding down, you can move the marker wherever you wish. This is useful when you have written a long text, and need to edit very specific portions of it.

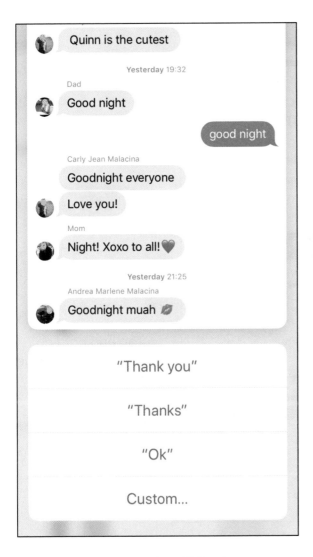

Figure 21.2 – Messages App: 3D Touch on a Thread

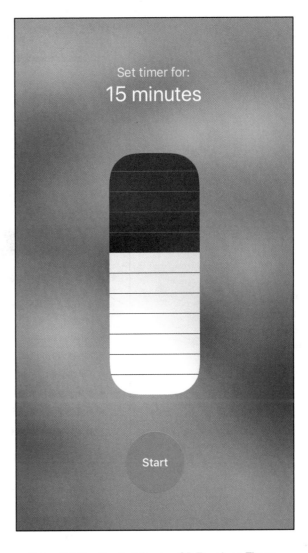

Figure 21.3 – Control Center: 3D Touch on Timer Icon

Copy and Paste

We have already covered how to copy a picture. As a reminder, you can do this generally by using 3D Touch on a photo and swiping up, and then tapping <u>Copy</u>. To paste it in text somewhere, double tap with your finger in the text area, and then tap on <u>Paste</u>.

To copy and paste text, find the text you want to copy and tap and hold on it. Now move the small marker dots left and right to select the exact portion of text you want to copy. Now tap the <u>Copy</u> box. You can paste the text by double tapping in a text box and then tapping <u>Paste</u>. (<u>Figure 21.4</u>)

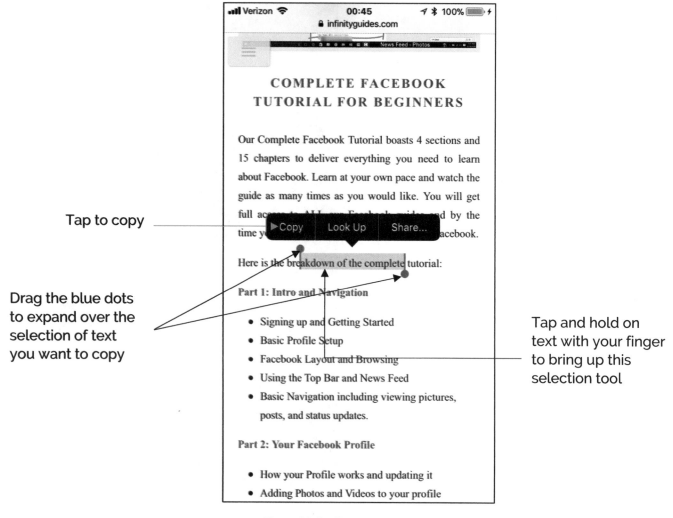

Figure 21.4 – Copy and Paste Text

Low Power Mode

One of the biggest complaints about the iPhone is the battery life. There are things you can do to improve the battery life of your iPhone, and one was already mentioned in this chapter (closing background apps). The other big way to preserve your battery life is by switching on Low Power Mode, which reduces power consumption temporarily. To do this, follow these steps:

1. Open Settings.
2. Tap Battery.
3. Tap the enable box next to Low Power Mode to enable it.
4. To turn it back off tap it again.

Customize the Control Center

A new feature to iOS 11 is the ability to customize the Control Center. You can choose which bottom buttons you want to appear. To do this:

1. Open <u>Settings</u>
2. Tap <u>Control Center</u>
3. You can remove buttons by tapping the <u>red minus sign</u> next to the app or function.
4. You can add buttons by tapping the <u>green plus sign</u> next to the app or function.

A special function you can add to the Control Center is Screen Recording. This allows you to record everything you are doing on your screen and it will save as a video in your Photos app.

Personal Hotspot

Your iPhone has the ability to become a personal hotspot, which in layman's terms is a device which can broadcast its internet connection to other devices. Using the personal hotspot feature is limited by your cellular provider, and some providers charge to use this service. So before you enable your personal hotspot, check with your cellular provider.

To enable the personal hotspot:

1. Open <u>Settings</u>.
2. Tap <u>Personal Hotspot</u>.
3. Enable Personal Hotspot by tapping on the <u>tabular icon</u> next to Personal Hotspot. When the tab is green personal hotspot is enabled.
4. Set a Wi-Fi password for devices to access your personal hotspot by tapping in the <u>Wi-Fi Password box</u> and creating a password.

A personal hotspot is a great way to create a Wi-Fi network for your other devices when Wi-Fi is not available. Be sure to turn Personal Hotspot off when you are done, as it uses significant battery power.

Siri Easter Eggs

As mentioned in the Siri chapter, you can say anything you want to Siri. Anything. You may even discover some Easter eggs while speaking to her. Try these: (Press and hold the <u>home button</u> to begin).

- How much wood could a woodchuck chuck is a woodchuck could chuck wood?
- What do you look like?
- I love you.
- I love my iPhone.
- I am tired.

Try some more yourself.

Chapter 22 – More Resources

This guide has covered all the beginner aspects of the iPhone. We have also covered many intermediate and advanced aspects, but there is still plenty more you can learn. Most notably, there is a lot to learn about specific apps. You can also learn more about Apple Music, iTunes, and social media on your iPhone.

Infinity Guides is an excellent resource for beginners, and on the Infinity Guides website you can find books, manuals, DVDs, and online courses made for beginners. The online courses can be especially helpful as most of them are about 30 minutes long and teach you through video instruction. I have created a short list of things you can learn with Infinity Guides for your reference.

www.infinityguides.com Content:

- Facebook for Beginners
- Twitter for Beginners
- Apple Music for Beginners
- Smartphones & Tablets for Beginners
- Instagram App for Beginners
- Snapchat App for Beginners
- iTunes for Beginners
- Mac Computer for Beginners
- Making your Computer Fast Again Tutorial

CONCLUSION

Thank you for taking the time to read this text. It is my hope that you feel much better about using your iPhone. I am confident that if you took the time to read this entire book, then you will have no problem using every aspect of your iPhone with ease. Continue to use this book as a reference when you need it. The table of contents can quickly lead you to your answer, and the appendixes can be especially helpful as well and I hope you use them.

I welcome your thoughts and feedback on this text, please come visit my Facebook page online at www.facebook.com/joemal. You can also tweet me @JoeMalacina on Twitter. I am often online answering questions from people who have read this text, and helping people with complex iPhone issues. As a last piece of advice, please remember your Apple ID, Apple ID password, and lock screen passcode. Forgetting even one of these, especially your lock screen passcode, can be a real headache.

Enjoy using your iPhone.

APPENDIX A – Additional Recommended Apps

- **560 The Answer** – A talk radio station's app that allows you to listen live and listen later
- **AirBnB** – Book lodging from regular people who put their vacation homes, rentals, condos, and dwellings up for short-term lodging.
- **Amazon** – Shop with Amazon's app. You can even order this book from Amazon.
- **Bible** – App for reading the bible
- **Clash of Clans** – World wide strategy and social game
- **Crossword** – Crossword puzzle game app
- **Fox Sports** – Official app for the Fox Sports channel
- **Expedia** – Travel app that allows you to compare and book travel accomodations
- **Facebook** – The Facebook social media app. Learn to use it at www.infinityguides.com
- **Facebook Messenger** – The messaging app for Facebook
- **Fandango** – Lookup movie show times, reviews, information, and local theaters
- **Flixster** – Movie ticketing app
- **Fox News** – The official app for the Fox News Channel
- **Google Chrome** – Alternative web browser
- **Google Maps** – Navigation app for GPS, directions, and places
- **Groupon** – Shopping app where you can purchase discounts and special deals
- **HD Wallpapers** – App for downloading wallpapers for your iPhone
- **iHeartRadio** – Radio app where you can listen to radio stations across the world and internet
- **Instagram** – Popular social media app for picture sharing. Learn to use it at www.infinityguides.com
- **McDonalds** – McDonald's official app which offers coupons and deals
- **Microsoft Office** – Apps for Word, Excel, and other Microsoft Office products
- **MLB App** – Official Major League Baseball app
- **MyFitnessPal** – Dieting and fitness app
- **Netflix** – Subscription app that allows you to watch TV shows and movies
- **NFL App** – Official National Football League app
- **OpenTable** – Dining app that allows you to book reservations and read reviews
- **Pages** – Word Processing app
- **Periscope** – Social Media app that allows you to view and view live videos
- **Radio.com** – Radio app that allows you to listen to various radio stations

- **Shazam** – App that can listen to and identify most songs
- **Shopular** – Shopping app that offers coupons and deals
- **SitorSquat** – Miscellaneous app where you can quickly find a public bathroom and read user reviews of bathrooms.
- **Sky Guide** – Fun app to view star constellations
- **Skype** – Video chat with your friends and family
- **Snapchat** – Social Media app especially popular among teens that allows you to send pictures and videos that disappear after a short time
- **Speedtest** – App that allows you to test your internet speed
- **SpotHero** – App that allows you to find and book parking
- **Target** – Shopping app for Target
- **The Weather Channel** – The always useful Weather Channel app
- **Twitter** – Very popular social media app where users can "tweet" messages to the world and to their followers. Learn more at www.infinityguides.com
- **Uber** – Ride-sharing app
- **VLC** – Video Player app
- **Wall Street Journal** – News app
- **Waze** – For Directions & GPS, with real-time traffic and user-generated alerts/
- **WebMD** – Health app for viewing various health information
- **Words with Friends** – A scrabble like game where you can compete with other people online
- **Yelp** – An app for reading and posting reviews of various places such as restaurants
- **Your Bank's App** – Always a good idea to have your bank's app so you can check balances, make deposits, and perform other banking activities.

APPENDIX B – Siri Examples

These are all examples of things you can say to Siri.

- What time is it?
- Show me restaurants around here
- Call *Contact Name*
- Send a text to *contact name*
- Open *app name*
- Check my e-mail
- Check my messages
- Do I have any appointments today?
- Check my battery life
- Send a text to *contact name*
- Tell *contact name* I am on my way in a text
- What movies are playing?
- Play *song name*
- Play *playlist name*
- Play *artist name*
- Remind me to wash the dishes tonight
- Email *contact name* about the trip
- Wake me up at 7 AM tomorrow.
- Note that I need to get my dog a new bone
- Turn on Airplane mode
- Decrease/Increase my brightness
- What is Apple's stock price?
- What is the address of *contact name*?
- Change my wallpaper
- Play a random song
- Where can I get a burger around here?

APPENDIX C – List of Common Functions

- **Add New Email to iPhone:** Settings -> Accounts & Passwords -> Add Account
- **Change Language:** Settings -> General -> Language & Region
- **Change Lock Screen Password or Fingerprints:** Settings -> Touch ID & Passcode
- **Change Ringtones:** Settings -> Sounds & Haptics
- **Change Wallpaper:** Settings -> Wallpapers
- **Check for iOS Updates:** Settings -> General -> Software Update
- **Completely Restore iPhone to Factory Default (WARNING: this will delete all of your iPhone data and bring it back to right out of the box status. DO NOT DO THIS unless you know what you are doing.):** Settings -> General -> Reset -> Erase all Content and Settings - > enter passwords
- **Connect to a Bluetooth Device:** Settings -> Bluetooth -> My Devices
- **Connect to a Wi-Fi Network:** Settings -> Wi-Fi -> Tap on Network -> Enter password -> Tap Join
- **Create New Text:** Messages -> Square and Pencil Icon
- **Join Apple Music:** Settings -> Music -> Join Apple Music
- **Set Default Search Engine:** Settings -> Safari -> Search Engine
- **Clear Your Internet History:** Settings -> Safari -> Clear History and Website Data
- **Sign in to your Apple ID:** Settings -> iTunes & App Store -> Apple ID
- **Switch to Military Time:** Settings -> General -> Date & Time -> 24 Hour Time
- **Turn Location Services On/Off:** Settings -> Privacy -> Location Services
- **Turn on Do Not Disturb:** Control Panel -> Moon Icon
- **Turn on iCloud Photo Library:** Settings -> Photos & Camera -> iCloud Photo Library
- **Turn Siri On/Off:** Settings -> Siri
- **Create a new E-mail:** Mail -> Square and Pencil Icon
- **Delete a Recent Call History:** Phone -> Recents Tab -> Swipe left over a recent call
- **Add Emoji's to Keyboard:** Settings -> General -> Keyboard -> Keyboards -> Add New Keyboard... -> Emoji

Check out more beginner's guides
and manuals at:

www.infinityguides.com